Baedeker

Madeira

www.baedeker.com

Verlag Karl Baedeker

SIGHTSEEING HIGHLIGHTS ★ ★

The »green pearl in the ocean« has so much to offer: rugged mountains, wild and romantic coastlines, unique laurisilva woods and fantastic flowers in bloom, picturesque villages and a charming capital – we have compiled a list of highlights you must not miss!

1 ★ ★ Funchal

The capital of Madeira with blossoming parks, interesting museums, a simple yet impressive cathedral, an attractive harbour and a quaint old town. Most visitors to Madeira stay in the hotel zone west of the town. ► page 130

2 ★ ★ Monte

The famous pilgrimage church houses the sarcophagus of the last Austrian emperor. One way to get here is the cable car from Funchal harbour, with a more bumpy ride by basket sled for the return leg. Take time out to wander through the Jardim Tropical in between. ► page 157

3 ★ ★ Cabo Girão

From Cabo Girão, almost 600m/2000ft high, the view down sheer cliffs on one of the world's most rugged coastlines can be a dizzying experience. ► page 122

4 ★ ★ Curral das Freiras

An adventurous little road leads along the mountainside to »Nun's Valley«; a drop of chestnut liqueur will help to settle the nerves on arrival. ► page 127

5 ★ ★ Pico do Arieiro

The road leads almost to the summit, so even less practised hikers should not have any problems and everyone can enjoy fantastic views of Madeira's magnificent mountain scenery. ► page 164

9 Porto Moniz

© Baedeker

8 Paul da Serra

▲ 6 Pico Ruivo

▲ 5 Pico do Arieiro

4 Curral das Freiras

7 Ponta de São Lourenço

2 Monte

1 Funchal

3 Cabo Girão

6 ✶✶ Pico Ruivo

Madeira's highest mountain can be reached from Pico do Arieiro in around 4 hours with reasonable stamina and suitable hiking equipment. The reward is an overwhelming panoramic view.
► page 164

7 ✶✶ Ponta de São Lourenço

Madeira's eastern peninsula is rough and rocky. The exposed rock fragments bear witness to the volcanic origins of the island – a play of colours in ochre, red, black and blue.   ► page 167

8 ✶✶ Paúl da Serra

Visitors can be forgiven for thinking they have landed in Scotland amidst the scraggy, green expanses – a different Madeira.   ► page 162

9 ✶✶ Porto Moniz

Lava poured and sizzled into the ocean

On Pico do Arieiro
Fantastic views await hikers on the heights of Madeira

Pilgrimage church in Monte
The azulejo scene enchants believers

and the wind and waves did their work over thousands of years, creating rock formations with practical uses – natural swimming pools.   ► page 172

BAEDEKER'S BEST TIPS

We have brought together the most interesting Baedeker tips in this book for you! Experience and enjoy Madeira at its very best.

☒ A musical introduction
Songs from Madeira on the CD entitled *Portugal Canta 2* ▶ page 46

☒ Treasures in lace
Where the most beautiful works in lace can be admired, past and present
▶ page 48

☒ On the trail of Columbus
Sailing along the south coast of Madeira in a replica of Columbus' ship is a pleasure for everyone. To find out where the ship is moored, turn to ▶ page 65

☒ Exotic fruit
Anonas, or cherimoyas, taste delicious. Just spit out the unbelievable number of brown pips. ▶ page 73

☒ Madeiran drinks at home
Everything you need to mix a poncha, in order to recreate that holiday feeling at home ▶ page 74

☒ Interesting new flavours
You can bring some chestnut liqueur home with you. Or how about some tasty fennel sweets from Curral das Freiras?
▶ page 89

☒ Nature lovers
Those who like to walk in the great outdoors will certainly not feel out of place on Madeira ▶ page 110

Delicate handicraft
This azulejo portrays women engaged in typical Madeira needlework

Madeira wine
The island's famous product

🚨 Exquisite drinks menu
Definitely worth trying: Madeira wines, rum and liqueurs are all on the list.
► page 119

🚨 High in the sky
The Madeira balloon at Funchal harbour: what better way to gain an initial overview? ► page 134

🚨 Sit back and enjoy
Perfect for a little break: the kiosk café in Funchal's municipal gardens
► page 139

🚨 Very british
Five o'clock tea at the famous Reid's Hotel with scones and all the trimmings – don't forget to wear a tie ► page 150

All aboard?
Basket sled may not be the cheapest form of transport, but it is certainly an unusual one!

A well-earned break
Between museums and other sites of interest, time for a short rest beneath shady trees

🚨 Sled ride with a difference
Fancy trying out a most unusual form of transport? Then don't miss out on a basket sled ride. ► page 159

The goat is not coming along on this levada hike
► page 100

BACKGROUND

Price categories

Hotels
Luxury: from 150 €
Mid-range: 75 – 150 €
Budget: below 75 €
For two people in a double room

Restaurants
Expensive: from 25 €
Moderate: 15 – 25 €
Inexpensive: up to 15 €
For a main course without drinks

PRACTICALITIES

*These charming straw houses in Santana
are known as Casas do Colmo*
► page 184

TOURS

SIGHTS FROM
A to Z

Background

A REGION AND ITS ISLAND INHABITANTS,
THE ECONOMY AND POLITICS,
FAMOUS PEOPLE, ARTS AND
CULTURE AND EVERYDAY LIFE:
BACKGROUND INFORMATION IN
CONCISE FORM FOR QUICK AND
EASY REFERENCE.

VERDANT PEARL IN THE OCEAN

... is just one of the decorative descriptions lent to this former bridgehead between the Old World and the New. »Daughter of the volcano«, »bride of the wind« or »island of eternal spring« are some of the names given to the floral island in the Atlantic, which lies almost twice as far from its Portuguese motherland as from the coast of mainland Africa.

Floral island in the Atlantic
»Public amusements are wholly lacking«, wrote the author of a *Handbook for Madeira* in 1885, while giving fulsome praise to the mild climate, magnificent landscape and generous hospitality of the islanders. Well, no change there, except that the recreational opportunities have increased beyond measure.

Madeira's average temperature of around 20°C/68°F, even in the November to February period, makes it a popular holiday destination for the winter months in Europe. A fantastic natural landscape, rich in vegetation and floral splendour throughout the year, attracts visitors searching for relaxation. Ancient laurisilva woodland and luxuriant gardens, white surf crashing on the coastline, deep valleys, rugged mountains and lush, green uplands create a fascinating ensemble. To the northeast, the neighbouring island of Porto Santo offers an interesting contrast, with over 9km/5mi of sandy beaches instead of floral resplendence and high mountains. The Ilhas Desertas to the southeast have been a designated nature reserve since 1990, off limits to visitors.

Fruitful
Funchal's market hall overflows with fruit and vegetables

A Hikers' Paradise

The pathways along the levadas, irrigation channels constructed over centuries, were not laid with hikers in mind, but for the levadeiros, the men who tend the levadas. However, they are perfectly suited to reconnoitring Madeira's original landscape and its diverse regions. A good head for heights and sturdy legs are helpful and the right equipment is advisable, as the steep mountainside is unguarded at

Impressive cultivation
*Even the smallest corner of land on
steep mountain slopes is put to good use*

Exquisite taste
*This special wine is one of the island's
most popular exports*

Romantic outlook
*Madeira is an island of magnificent viewing points –
this one on the northeast coast*

Handmade quality
Extraordinary hours of labour go into fine Madeiran embroidery

Wildlife under protection
The Ilhas Desertas, a nature reserve for the last monk seals, are closed to visitors

Artistic tradition
Many a church wall is decorated from top to bottom with traditional azulejos

some points, or it may be necessary to balance on the levada wall. The reward for such endeavours comes in the form of spectacular views!

Funchal

The capital city of Funchal, located on the south coast, is the cultural and tourist centre of the island. Although it is the seat of government, centre for shopping, a bishop's see, a university town and a port, the site of engaging museums, tropical gardens and amusements, this is no overcrowded metropolis. Nevertheless, in the western part of town, a veritable hotel zone has developed, whilst new settlements have crept up the slopes of Funchal Bay and traffic has drastically increased in the city centre. The key spots are easily reachable on foot, and a hot-air balloon at the harbour is a good way of getting one's bearings. New roads, constructed in recent years with the assistance of EU funding, now connect Funchal with relative ease to previously remote regions such as the north coast or the western promontory of the island. There is much worth discovering in those regions too: welcoming fishing communities with small harbours, village churches that glory in Baroque opulence, small thatched houses, fortifications to thwart pirates, mansions known as quintas – at the heart of magnificent parks, terraced fields with grapevines for the famous Madeira wine, banana plantations and lava caves. Traditional handicrafts live on in ornate Madeira embroidery

and basketry. Pictures made from azulejos – ceramic tiles – adorn façades, whilst plaster mosaics of light and dark stones add atmosphere to Funchal and many other places on the island.

A fine residence
Quinta do Palheiro outside Funchal is one of the most attractive Madeiran estates

If there were a guest book for Madeira, it would read like a who's who of the noble, rich and beautiful classes. Winston Churchill whiled away his time drawing and painting in the harbour of Câmara de Lobos, George Bernard Shaw sampled the delights of the tango against a tropical backdrop, and Empress Elisabeth I of Austria came here to escape the cold Viennese winter. Discover your very own, personal slice of paradise on Madeira, the island of eternal spring!

Facts

Where did the name Madeira come from? Who really discovered it? What grows here, which creatures crawl or fly over the island? What is the story of the azulejos, seen not only on walls and façades, but also on church roofs and towers? Where does Columbus figure in the history of Madeira?

Natural Environment

The Madeira archipelago (Arquipélago da Madeira) is situated in the Atlantic, some 500km/300mi to the west of the Moroccan coast. The main island of Madeira rises out of the Atlantic Ocean from a depth of 4000–5000m/13,000–16,000ft to as high as 1862m/6100ft above sea level (Pico Ruivo, »Red Peak«). Also part of the archipelago are the island of Porto Santo at a distance of 43km/26mi, the Ilhas Desertas –

DID YOU KNOW ...?

■ With an area of 741 square kilometres/ 286 square miles, the archipelago of Madeira is roughly half as large as Greater London.

Ilhéu Chão, Deserta Grande and Ilhéu do Bugio – approximately 20km/13mi southeast, and the five tiny Ilhas Selvagens (covering approx. 4 sq km/1.5 sq mi together), much further south, closer to the Canary Isles.

The first impression for newcomers to Madeira is striking: black and brown lava cliffs, dark basalt and light volcanic tuff dominate the island, where fissured rock faces climb almost vertically from the sea in a landscape of sharp ridges, abruptly plunging gorges and forbidding rocky cliffs, such as the 580m/1900ft-high Cabo Girão. Cooled lava streams at Porto Moniz and the lava drips in the caves at São Vicente are also noteworthy. Seawater and wind have shaped the highly unusual northeastern promontory of Madeira, Ponta de São Lourenço, hollowing out the volcanic tuff stone over the centuries to form gradually disintegrating caves, the characteristic »tafonis«. Solidified lava has been hewn into sharp-edged cliffs, often inaccessible to all except to the seagulls that breed there.

Birth of fire

Madeira, Porto Santo and the Ilhas Desertas, together with the Azores, the Cape Verde islands and the Canaries, comprise the Macaronesia Islands, otherwise known as the **mid-Atlantic volcanic islands**. Today, they lie far from the volcanically active Atlantic Ridge at the border of the Atlantic Ocean's crust. Between 135 and 160 million years ago, however, as the Atlantic Ocean gradually began to open up, the submerged volcanic ridge exactly followed the line along which the Macaronesian Islands now reach up from the waters. In actual fact, the islands visible today only appeared above sea level much later, some 10 to 40 million years ago. At first, beneath the ocean, surface rifts and chasms opened, out of which basaltic magma erupted, created vast bodies of basaltic lava, breccias and so forth. Ten to twenty million years ago, these **undersea volcanoes** rose above the ocean surface, forming volcanic islands with basalt stacks, cinder cones and lava streams. Saltwater and the elements

The formation of the Madeira archipelago

← *Many traders on Madeira made a handsome profit from sugarcane*

Madeira Archipelago Map

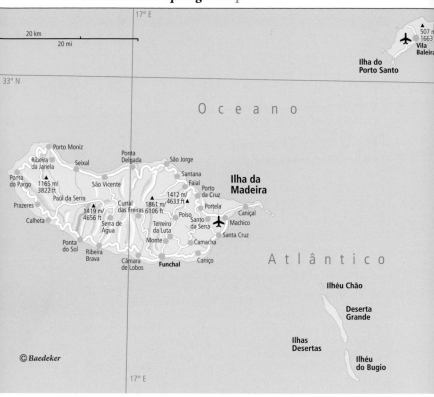

weathered the young volcanic islands as the process of erosion began. Around seven million years ago, a renewed phase of violent volcanic activity saw Porto Santo rise above sea level.

Current situation Volcanic activity in the region of the Madeira archipelago has since decreased considerably, but is far from over. In 2001, scientists from the Meteor research group discovered and mapped a submarine volcanic ridge structure approximately 50km/30mi west of Madeira. It is conjectured that a so-called »**hot spot**« exists in the area of the Madeira archipelago, periodically responsible for fresh outbreaks of volcanic activity. Here, the sea bed drifts over a fixed magma flue (»hot spot«), which penetrates the earth's crust like a welding torch, piling up huge cones of volcanic matter on the ocean floor. The Madeira »hot spot« has now been charted in the region of the Madeira archipelago, tracing the movement of the African Plate as it shifts northeast, towards Europe.

The spine of the main island of Madeira is a mountain range of jagged and precipitous ridges, stretching from east to west. In the western part of the island lies the Paúl da Serra tableland; to the east is the smaller plateau of Santo António da Serra. On the north and south slopes of the central chain, sheer rock faces surround basins which then open into the ocean as deep incisions or gorges. Especially on the northern coast, it is easy to see the frequent alternation of ash and lava strata. The coasts of Madeira are steep and rocky; narrow expanses of sand can only be found on a few erstwhile lava streams flowing into the ocean. Porto Santo, by way of contrast, consists mainly of sandy uplands with volcanic cones as high as 517m/1696ft. The volcanic rock of the Ilhas Desertas reaches a height of 479m/1570ft. Attempts to put this dry and infertile land to agricultural use were swiftly abandoned: hence the name meaning »Deserted Islands«.

Terrain

> **? DID YOU KNOW ...?**
>
> ■ ... that the word »lombo«, which occurs in so many place names on Madeira, means »ridge«? Most settlements thus named are indeed situated on a hillcrest or in the upper regions of a gorge.

Climate

Madeira owes its lush vegetation to a climate that is markedly oceanic and, as a result of its low latitude, warm. Depressions from northern latitudes determine the winter weather, whilst the northeast trade winds dominate the summer half of the year, creating stark **climatic differences** between the windward side to the north and the lee side to the south. This is caused by the formation of clouds, as northerly winds bring damp air masses which gather around the mountains, primarily in the mornings. From around noon, the air masses warm up and begin to rise, thus influencing the weather on the southern part of the island.

Island of »eternal spring«

On the northern side, where the trade winds are caught on the mountainsides, rainfall is heavy, especially in the winter months. On the southern side of the island, annual precipitation averages are much lower. Apart from the remarkably dry months of July and August, showers can fall at any moment on Madeira, with longer periods of rainfall quite possible further inland. The annual mean temperature on the island is also determined by its geographical location at 32° latitude. Even in winter, it is rare for the thermometer to drop below 18°C/64°F in the lower regions of the island during the day. Snowfall is a distinct possibility in the uplands, but the snow never settles. There is a difference between the north and south: whilst the annual mean temperature in Funchal is 18.2°C/64.5°F, the damper northern side at Ponta Delgada registers just 17.4°C/63°F. Occasional masses of hot air from the Sahara make their way to Madeira; these

Precipitation and temperatures

The trade winds bring the clouds: view from the Paúl da Serra plateau

winds can be unpleasant, bringing not only hot air with them but desert sand as well.

Water temperatures vary between 14°C/57°F in March and around 22°C/71°F at the height of summer.

Flora and Fauna

Natural vegetation

When João Gonçalves Zarco and Tristão Vaz Teixeira set foot on Madeira in 1419 and were confronted with a mountainous, densely forested and impassable island, they christened the place with a name befitting the terrain: **Madeira means wood in Portuguese**. The discoverers initially settled on the flatter neighbouring island of Porto Santo, using it as a base from which to explore the main island. Early Portuguese settlers opted for **fire clearance** as their preferred method of claiming the land. According to contemporary documentation, the fires burned for seven years, with little remaining of the primeval forest which had grown over centuries. This destroyed the majority of the indigenous flora and fauna.

Vegetation today

»Flor do Oceano« – »Flower of the Ocean« – is what the Portuguese call their island in the Atlantic today. The vegetation of Madeira is nowadays characterized by a **tropical abundance** of splendid and useful plants from all corners of the earth, thanks to its mild climate, plentiful winter rainfall and the artificial irrigation system of the levadas, which channel water from the mountains to the fields and gardens along the coast. As well as pine and European broadleaf, countless evergreen trees and shrubs of tropical and subtropical origin thrive here, such as palms, monkey puzzle, hickory, cork oak, camphor and fig trees, papaya, palm lily, yuccas, medlar, mimosa eucalyptus, bamboo, papyrus plants, cyatheales and agave. Many streets are lined with blossoming hydrangeas, usually blue in colour, agapanthus in white and blue, and belladonna lilies (Brunsvigia rosea), originally from South Africa. **Orchids** are cultivated in many varieties in orchid gardens. A visit to such a cultivation centre is commonly a disappointment, as the various species bloom at different times and are relatively unspectacular in appearance out of season. Orchids are, however, hugely popular as enduring and low-maintenance souvenirs.

In the gardens of Funchal, often contained within high walls, an enchanting floral richness can be enjoyed in winter and more especially in spring: roses, camellias, rhododendrons, azaleas, pelargoniums, begonias, bignonias, daturas, bougainvillea, wisteria and many more. Indigenous to Mexico, the poinsettia now flowers prodigiously on Madeira. The **strelitzia**, introduced to Madeira from South Africa in 1778, can be found in almost every garden and is grown in fields for export. Its striking blossoms, resembling birds' heads, are carefully packed as popular souvenirs.

?   DID YOU KNOW ...?

- ... how the strelitzia (Strelitzia reginae) got its name? It was thought up in 1774 by a German gardener named Andreas Auge, in honour of Charlotte of Mecklenburg-Strelitz, Queen of England as consort to George III.

Crop plants

Upwards of 800m/2600ft, the prevailing **eucalyptus woods** have been developed through reforestation. Both species, Eucalyptus globulus and Eucalyptus ficifolia, originate from the Australian continent and were only exported to Europe in the 20th century. The eucalyptus tree is highly valued as a rapidly renewable wood with many uses. A hike through the forests is all the more pleasant when the inimitable eucalyptus scent fills the air, a eucalyptus twig in the car is a natural air freshener, and tasty sweets can be manufactured from its essential oils. The downside: eucalyptus draws large quantities of water from the earth.

At the time of Madeira's discovery, **Florence fennel** (Foeniculum dulce) was widespread on the island. The name of Funchal is a reminder of the fact: Portuguese seafarers who landed in the bay are said to have been so beguiled by its aroma that they named the town after it. Today fennel is used as seasoning in cooking, and also in making sweets.

The most important **crops** are, nevertheless, vines, potatoes and bananas. Aloe vera is gaining in economic significance as well.

Protected by UNESCO: laurisilva forest

Only a small area of the original laurisilva forest, so prevalent in the Mesozoic age and in the Mediterranean too, has survived on Madeira, the Canaries, the Azores and Cape Verde Islands. In 1999 the woodland was declared a UNESCO **World Heritage site**, forming the heart of a nature reserve. The laurel woods contain sizeable numbers of Madeira laurel (Laurus indica), stinkwood or till trees (Oreodaphne foetens) and laurel or Canary laurel (Laurus barbusano). Above 1000m/3300ft, Canary Islands juniper (Juniperus cedrus), wild olive trees (Olea maderensis), above 1500m/4900ft Scotch heather (Erica scoparia) and shield fern (Polystichum falcinellum) can be found.

The **dragon tree** (Dracaena draco), probably the island's most distinctive indigenous plant, has largely disappeared as a consequence of the multiple uses for its wood. More recently, it has increasingly been planted in parks and gardens for decorative purposes.

Animal kingdom

Of the many varieties in Madeira's **bird kingdom**, only 14 or 15 breeds are natives of the island. Some 200 bird species live or breed on Madeira, including birds of prey such as buzzards and falcons, along with canaries, the Madeiran wood pigeon and petrels. Magpies, chaffinches, common buzzards, the rare Madeira laurel pigeon and the Madeira firecrest, a member of the wren family – also known as »bisbis« on account of its characteristic call – all inhabit the laurel forest. These dwindling bird populations in the laurel forest are the very ones threatened with extinction.

The highest share of indigenous species can be found amongst the **insects**. In adapting, many have lost the ability to fly. The poisonous wolf spider (Geolycosa ingens) is endemic to the island of Deserta Grande, a nature reserve with no access for tourists. The only **reptile species** is the Madeira wall lizard, which likes to feed on ripe fruit in gardens and plantations, in spite of the efforts of farmers to prevent it from doing so. Snakes do not live on the islands. Bats are the only indigenous mammals.

Introduced farm and wild animals

Cattle, horses, donkeys, goats, pigs, sheep, hedgehogs and rabbits, as well as rats and mice, were all brought to the archipelago by man. Rainbow trout farms have also been introduced, the trout reared in

»Pride of Madeira« is the name given to these beautiful flowers, →
seen in many places on the island

Black scabbard fish from the depths of the ocean

hatcheries (in Ribeiro Frio, for example) and later released into streams for anglers' enjoyment.

Fish The waters around Madeira are very deep, so fish are not especially common. This is not a habitat suitable for the marine life found in brackish or shallower water elsewhere in the world, such as mussels or crabs. Tuna, monkfish, redfish and octopus live in the waters surrounding Madeira. The most important edible fish of Madeira is the **black scabbard fish** (»espada preta«), an eel-like, scaleless deep-sea fish up to 2m/6ft in length and found only around Madeira and off the coast of Japan. It lives over 1000m/3300ft below sea level, climbing to just 800m/2600ft at night, when it may be caught on long fishing lines. In the service of gastronomy, it suffers a gruesome death: as water pressure decreases the closer it gets to the surface, its air bladder, gills and eyes burst and its slimy, scaleless skin turns black. Hauled upwards, the colourful iridescence it displays in its natural habitat is lost, with only the black dyes surviving.

A large **monk seal** (Monachus monachus, ►Baedeker Special, p. 120) population, now almost extinct, used to thrive in the bay of Câmara de Lobos and was also prevalent around the Canary Islands, on the northwest coast of Africa and the Mediterranean in former times. To ensure the colony's survival, as well as to protect the marine flora and fauna of the Madeira archipelago, **nature reserves** have been created, also encompassing the Ilhas Desertas and Ilhas Selvagens. Immediately off Madeira, the Ponta do Garajau at the eastern side of the Bay of Funchal was given partial protection in 1986 and fishing has been heavily restricted. Diving equipment is necessary to explore the magnificent underwater regions of the nature reserve. Grouper can be seen here, whilst manta also venture into these waters. Through the efforts of the local population, the strip of coast at Rocha do Navio has been designated a conservation area, offering a potential habitat to monk seals.

Today, roughly two thirds of Madeira has been awarded nature reserve status for the protection of endemic fauna and flora.

Politics · Population · Economy

The island of Madeira is divided into eleven **municipalities** (concelhos), in turn subdivided into 53 **parishes** (freguesias). Funchal, the only town of any notable size on Madeira, is the seat of the political leadership, legislative organs and administration. Madeira's **governing body** consists of a regional presidentand a regional government, with political decisions taken by the 55-member regional assembly. The neighbouring island of Porto Santo, forming a twelfth parish, enjoys a degree of independence.

Political structure

Madeira belongs to Portugal Since the so-called Revolution of the Carnations of 1974, the archipelago has maintained a **high level of political autonomy**, anchored in the Portuguese constitution and the statute of the Autonomous Region. The sovereignty of Portugal is represented by a minister of the republic, who works together with the region's institutions. Madeira is also seat of the European Council for Environmental Law.

Relationship to Portugal

Since 1976, the Social Democratic Party (PSD) has continuously provided the members of parliament. In spite of the »social democratic« tag, the PSD is politically right of centre. Most mayors also come from the ranks of the PSD.

Political parties

On account of its more favourable climate, the south coast of Madeira is more densely populated than the rest of the island. Funchal alone with some 130,000 inhabitants represents **half of the population**. As the island's main tourist centre, Funchal offers greater potential to earn money than elsewhere on Madeira.

The extended family used to be a typical feature of the Madeiran population structure, but today families with many children are becoming rarer. **Population growth is stagnating** in line with Portugal in general.

Population

Facts and Figures Madeira

Lisbon

Madeira

© Baedeker

Archipelago
► Madeira Archipelago
(Portuguese: Arquipélago da Madeira)
► Main islands: Madeira, Porto Santo,
Ilhas Desertas (Ilhéu Chão, Deserta
Grande, Ilhéu do Bugio), Ilhas
Selvagens

Location
► between 33° 07' and 30° 01' N latitude
and 15° 51' and 17° 15' W longitude

Distances (from Funchal)
► to Lisbon: approx. 1000km/600mi
► to the coast of Morocco:
approx. 500km/300mi
► to the Canaries: approx. 450km/280mi

Area
► 741 sq km/286 sq mi (Madeira)

Extent
► East – west: approx. 57km/35mi
► North – south: approx. 22km/14mi
► Highest elevation:
Pico Ruivo, 1862m/6108ft

Population
► approx. 244,000, including 4500 on
Porto Santo

Language
► Portuguese

Religion
► 94 % Roman Catholic

Government
► Madeira Autonomous Region
► Funchal is the seat of the regional
assembly, the regional president and
the administration.

Economy
► The most important source of income is
tourism: more than 800,000 visitors to
Madeira per annum. In 2004, the
number of German tourists exceeded
that of the British for the first time,
with both groups arriving in greater
number than Portuguese guests from
the mainland.
► Most important export items: wine and
bananas.

Transport
► Airport: Santa Catarina or Aeroporto da
Madeira

Tourism may be on the increase, but this cannot disguise the fact
that young people, in particular those with good qualifications, are
faced with limited career opportunities. This is borne out by a **high**

migration rate, with many young adults heading for the Portuguese mainland or other European countries on completing their education. Popular overseas destinations include Brazil and Venezuela as Portuguese and Spanish-speaking countries respectively, as well as South Africa, USA and Canada.

At the **university** in Funchal, founded in 1988, the emphasis is on natural sciences, for example marine biology; degrees in art and design or music and languages are also possible.

The Roman Catholic Church is gradually losing the great influence it once held over the population, especially with regard to the young people living in and around Funchal. Outside the capital, the church still plays a major role in the lives of village communities. Festive religious processions are undoubtedly among the highlights of the year.

As elsewhere, there is a growing discrepancy on Madeira between the old ...

Economy

An important factor in the development of the economy on Madeira has been the support of the **European Union**, which pumped considerable funds into the island. The road network has been extended and modernized at great expense. EU aid is also proving effective in agriculture.

There has been a sharp decline in **cattle breeding** overall. Pig husbandry has gained somewhat in importance as a consequence of the increasing number of hungry tourists. A visit to the market confirms the rich variety of plant life

... and the young

on Madeira. As crops can be grown all year round and harvested several times a year, the island is completely self-sufficient in the provision of **fruit and vegetables** and is, moreover, able to export surplus agricultural produce. The only fruit and vegetables imported are brought in to add to the already rich diversity on offer.

Of all the agricultural products of Madeira, **Madeira wine** has the longest tradition. The island's volcanic origins furnish the vine with soils low in lime, complemented by sufficient moisture and plenty of sunshine. The secret of this famous sweet wine lies in the solera refining process, with the addition of brandy and plenty of time for ageing (▶ Baedeker Special, p. 70). As in northern Portugal, vines in Madeira are grown to head height, leaving the area below free for other agricultural produce, such as sweet potatoes or other vegetables.

The second most important produce after wine is the **potato**. **Bananas** are cultivated on the south coast and harvested throughout the year. The smaller, plainer varieties tend to be sweeter, with a more intense flavour than the larger ones. Fish with grilled banana is a speciality of Madeiran cuisine.

Topographical disadvantages Since time immemorial, the agricultural prosperity of Madeira has been hindered by the fact that only a third of the island is cultivable. The small fields on the countless **terraces** are still largely tilled by hand even now; machinery here is barely practicable. As fewer and fewer people are willing to take on this arduous labour for a paltry financial reward, the economic importance of farming is waning – as it is right across Europe.

Fishing Fishing is not of any great significance on Madeira. Again, topography is decisive in this respect: the ocean bed off the coast of Madeira falls away sharply and the deeper waters are sparsely populated by fish. Tuna, mackerel and the black scabbard fish are the most common catch, along with monkfish and redfish. Up until 1981, the village of Caniçal lived from whaling, before international protests put an end to what had been an economically important trade for the whole of Portugal.

Industry and crafts Industry is scarce on Madeira, not least as a result of the topographical conditions, which are not conducive to large production facilities. Some smaller firms are located around Funchal, but they manufacture products almost exclusively for the island itself. Eastern Madeira is home to a small industrial zone outside Caniçal. **Embroidery** has a long tradition on the island, with tablecloths in countless varieties, ornately decorated napkins and handkerchiefs or tapestries exported

These sweet fruits are popular on Madeira and the world over

all over the world. For many families on Madeira, embroidery makes an indispensable contribution to the household income. More than 30,000 women are engaged in embroidery today, the majority of them working from home.

Camacha is the main hub of the **basketry** trade. This handicraft has roughly as long a history on Madeira as embroidery. As machinery cannot be used in the weaving process, each item is unique.

Tourism

The annual influx of well over 800,000 holidaymakers secures close to 7000 jobs in the island's hotels, with an additional 15,000 directly related to tourism. The hotel sector alone accounts for approximately 10% of the region's gross output, concentrated primarily in and around Funchal. Most visitors today, as has always been the case, hail from Great Britain, Germany and the Portuguese mainland. **The most vital sector**

By the mid-19th century, Madeira was rapidly becoming a popular holiday destination. The mild climate attracted people with pulmonary ailments or gout, hopeful of curing their condition. They were joined by many members of princely or royal courts and the moneyed classes. Ultimately, Madeira was regarded as a decidedly **upper-class holiday domicile** during the cold and wet winters of central Europe. The first hotels on Madeira, including the distinguished Reid's **History**

Palace Hotel, (►Baedeker Special, p. 148), were built in the late 19th century. Arriving by boat was both expensive and time-consuming, but the opening of the airport in 1964 rectified the situation and ensured the continuous development of Madeira tourism. Since then, the number of hotel beds has multiplied to the extent that Madeira now has some 25,000 beds in over 150 hotels and numerous smaller hostels, whilst Porto Santo has around 1500 beds. Madeira is renowned for a high proportion of superior hotels – 4-star establishments are in the majority.

Outlook for the 21st century ► The regional government intends to promote individual tourism more heavily than mass tourism. Furthermore, efforts are being made to make the island more interesting to younger holidaymakers and improve its image accordingly. Meanwhile, the congress and conference capacity is being increased, as the expansion of the congress centre in Funchal demonstrates; a glance at the prospectus of one of the larger hotels confirms that many are perfectly equipped to cater for such events. Physical well-being has again become a focal point for guests in the 21st century: many hotels offer a wide range of health spa facilities.

Transport

Pathways and road network The topography of Madeira has been a perennial problem in terms of establishing an infrastructure of roads to all corners of the island. A network of simple cobbled lanes proved the best means of negotiating the precipitous terrain, with gorges traversed by narrow stone bridges. Tight, winding roads connected one settlement to the next. More recently, wider roads have been constructed, primarily through EU funding, in some cases connected by miles-long tunnels. Improvements to the communications network are also visible in the expansion of local transport services. Most, if not all, parts of the island can now be reached relatively comfortably by bus.

Unusual means of transport The typical Madeira pathways and road conditions saw some rather unusual forms of conveyance or transport in the 17th and 18th centuries: not only the more wealthy Madeirans were carried by »**rede**«, a hammock slung on two poles. Tourists also took advantage of the service, even to ascend Madeira's highest mountain, Pico Ruivo. The **palanquin**, a board fixed to a wooden or iron frame, was used to carry people and goods of all kinds. The brace of palanquin bearers needed to be strong, sturdy on their feet and have a good head for heights. Finally, the »**carro de bois**« was a sled pulled by a pair of oxen, invented by an Englishman, Major Buckley, in 1848 and far more comfortable than the alternatives. Members of high society covered their »carros de bois« with cloth to keep out the elements. Relics from a distant bygone age are the **basket sleds**, once a usual means of transport from Monte down to Funchal. Today they are essentially little more than a successful tourist attraction, demonstrating the ancient form of transport over a shorter distance (►fig. p. 5 and ►Sights from A to Z, Monte).

Madeira's international airport is situated approximately 18km/11mi east of Funchal. The first planes landed on Madeira in 1921 – seaplanes in those days, alighting on Funchal Bay. Later, the small NATO airbase on Porto Santo, built in 1960, came into use. Travellers were then ferried to Madeira by boat. Ideas about constructing an airport on Madeira's only high plateau, Paúl da Serra, remained just that, on account of the frequent fog there.

The present airport was opened in 1964. High mountains alongside the runway and unpredictable downwinds earned the airport the accolade of being one of Europe's most challenging. For many years, the airstrip was a mere 1800m/2000yd long, hence the nickname of »aircraft carrier«. The runway has subsequently been ex-

Road of adventure ...

tended to accommodate the increase in air traffic: since the summer of 2000, larger planes have been able to land here. One section reaches out into the ocean, built on columns over the water. Pilots now enjoy easier conditions for take-off and landing thanks to the 3000m/3250yd runway and an improved angle of approach. Propeller planes still land at the NATO airfield on Porto Santo.

History

Although there may be no conclusive evidence as to who really discovered Madeira, the official history of the island begins in the year 1418, when Gonçalves Zarco and Vaz Teixeira cast an inquiring eye in its direction from Porto Santo. They did not actually set foot on the island until the following year.

Conquest and Colonization

1351	Madeira makes its first appearance on a nautical chart.
1419	The first Portuguese land on Madeira.
From 1440	Malvasia grape and sugarcane

The question of who can lay claim to the discovery of Madeira is still open to debate (► Baedeker Special, p. 34). Madeira was officially plotted for the first time on a Florentine nautical chart in 1351. However, the first colonists only settled on the island some 70 years later. It was at this time that the younger son of King João I, the Infante **Henry the Navigator** (1394–1460), organized voyages of exploration to find a sea route to foreign lands such as India and develop the spice trade. On one such expedition, the Portuguese captains João Gonçalves Zarco and Tristão Vaz Teixeira landed on the neighbouring island, which they named Porto Santo, in 1418, claiming it for the Portuguese Crown. On their return, they reported back to the prince on the existence of a much larger island in the vicinity. In 1419, Henry dispatched the two once again, this time accompanied by the nobleman Bartolomeu Perestrello, who established a base on Porto Santo whilst Zarco and Teixeira took possession of the adjacent, uninhabited island for Portugal, giving it the name »Madeira« (wood), a reference to the dense woodland they found there.

»Wood Island«

Due to their favourable geostrategic location, Madeira and Porto Santo were earmarked for development as **supply stations for Portuguese expedition ships**. In 1423, the first colonists settled in the bays of Machico and Câmara de Lobos and set about reclaiming the impenetrable terrain of Madeira by means of fire clearance. Sometimes the fires got out of hand; on one occasion, so the story goes, the settlers were forced to flee to their ships and wait on board for two days until the flames had died down. After seven years, or thereabouts, the virgin forest had been virtually destroyed.

Fire clearance

In 1440, Henry the Navigator had the first Malvasia vines brought to Madeira from Crete, and rapid growth of **viniculture** ensued. **Sugarcane** also thrived, and before long the wood island was renowned throughout Europe for the excellent quality of its sugar. The arduous labour on the sugarcane plantations and in the sugar mills as well as the construction of the terraced fields and irrigation channels (levadas; ► Baedeker Special, p. 160) was carried out by slaves, initially drawn from the aboriginal people of the Canaries – not wholly correctly known as Guanches – and later from the west coast of Africa.

Agricultural basis

← »... experience the delirium of the coast down, over the polished stones, in a wicker sled.« (Winston Churchill)

Discoverers are always a good model for monuments as they gaze into the distance. The statue of Zarco in Funchal is a case in point

A DEBATABLE DISCOVERY

1419 is the year noted in history books for the conquest of Madeira – but when was the archipelago actually discovered? A sea chart dated 1351 already plots the island in the Atlantic. More mysterious by far is the legend that a pair of English lovers discovered Madeira.

The two Portuguese captains, **João Gonçalves Zarco** and **Tristão Vaz Teixeira**, commissioned by Henry the Navigator to explore the oceans, first set eyes on Madeira in 1418 – having been blown off course, so the story goes – when they landed on the uninhabited island of Porto Santo. A second expedition took them to Madeira. They took some time to pluck up the courage to set foot on the larger island. Above all, the dramatic cloud cover which sometimes hung over the landscape led Zarco to believe that this could indeed be the »Mouth of Hell«.

Sea chart of 1351

The Madeiran archipelago was first plotted on a Florentine nautical chart as early as 1351. Madeira is marked as »I. do lolegname«, which may be derived from the Arabic »el aghnam«, meaning »**wood island**«. Porto Santo (»Porto Séo«) and the Ilhas Desertas (»I. deserte«) are also represented. It is a matter of speculation whether Italian sailors who regularly made their way to the Canaries, Arab seamen or even Phoenicians, Carthaginians or Romans were aware of the archipelago.

The legend of Robert Machyn and Anne Dorset

When historical questions remain open, the scope for myths is great. The best-known and perhaps the most intriguing legend relates that the English nobleman **Sir Robert Machyn** (or Machin) who, in 1346 – five years before Madeira appeared on the sea chart mentioned above – was exiled from his homeland for an undisclosed offence. Accompanied by his lover, a certain **Anne Dorset**, who

was apparently below his social rank, he set out for Portugal. A storm dragged his ship off course, forcing him to land on Madeira in the bay where **Machico** now stands – its name derived from the Englishman's own, so the legend would have us believe. Machyn and a servant reconnoitred the island. When they returned after three days, ship and crew had vanished. Only Anne remained, but she died a few days later. Robert buried her under a wooden cross and built a chapel in her memory. He and his servant then constructed a boat, set sail and landed on the coast of Africa – at the exact same point where his renegade comrades, captured by Moors, were now stranded. Cast into the same dungeons as his crew, Robert furiously set upon the traitors. The King of Fez heard the story, thus learning of the existence of Madeira. However, neither the Moorish ruler nor the Castilian monarch to whom Robert was dispatched showed any interest in the uninhabited island.

Variations on a theme

There are numerous variations on the legend of Madeira's discovery. Some depict Anne as a noble lady and Robert as a lowly knight. One particularly touching version has Zarco, aware of the lovers' tragic fate, finding the wooden cross which marked the spot where Anne and Robert were buried – both having perished on the island in this account. The crew, the narrative goes on, had etched their story into the cross, concluding with a request: should Christians ever happen to find the spot on the island, they should erect a chapel here. Zarco respected their pious wish and built a small house of worship, which was then completely destroyed by a flood in 1803.

Special Status in the Colonial Empire

1497	Funchal is declared capital of the island and Madeira is accorded special status.
16th century	Pirates are attracted by the island's riches.
1580–1640	Madeira passes into Spanish hands.

Sugar loaves in the coat of arms

In 1497 King Manuel I annexed the archipelago into his kingdom, declaring Funchal the capital of Madeira. In 1508 Funchal was granted city status, thus earning the right to present its own coat of arms: it depicts five sugar loaves, a reference to Madeira as a major supplier of sugar. In 1514, as the local population approached 5000, Funchal's cathedral was consecrated and a bishop appointed. The diocese of Funchal incorporated all of Portugal's occupied territories in Africa and Asia, all the way to Japan.

The Madeirans become Portuguese

The sugar boom on Madeira ended as early as the beginning of the 16th century, the soil having effectively been drained of its nutrients. Furthermore Europe's biggest supplier of sugar was facing severe competition from another Portuguese colony, Brazil. Madeira, however, profited from its special status in the Portuguese colonial empire: from 1497 onwards, the island's inhabitants were no longer classed as colonials, but as Portuguese citizens. This allowed them to concentrate on **self-sufficient farming** unlike their colonial counterparts, who were restricted to monoculture in the interests of profit and were dependent on the motherland for their own needs. As state nationals, the inhabitants of Madeira enjoyed another privilege: all overseas products had to be shipped via Portuguese ports. Instead of manufacturing their own sugar, the Madeirans made money through interim storage and by selling Brazilian sugar. Many owners of large estates switched their attention from sugarcane cultivation to grapevines. Madeira shipped its sought-after wine (▶Baedeker Special, p. 70) to Portugal and its colonies overseas, and later straight to England and the British colonies. In 1643, Portugal's King João IV issued a decree that would prove highly lucrative for Madeira, whereby every ship bound for Brazil first had to stop at Funchal to load foodstuffs. Ships from other seafaring states also docked at Madeira before crossing the Atlantic, taking on board provisions and supplies – and filling the coffers of the islanders.

? DID YOU KNOW ...?

■ ... that Christopher Columbus was also involved in the sugar trade? Between 1479 and 1482, according to the perhaps not entirely reliable legend, he lived on Porto Santo, married, incidentally, to Filipa Perestrello, daughter of the first Portuguese governor.

Wealth attracts predators, and merchant ships repeatedly found **Pirates**
themselves attacked by pirates. Buccaneers also attempted to land on
the island. In 1513, King Manuel I decreed that the São Lourenço
fortress be constructed to protect Funchal, bolstered by an efficient
early warning system: as pirates invariably approached from the
north or east, they were easier to
spot from Porto Santo than from
the main island. Stacks of wood
which had been piled up in advance for such eventualities were
ignited to warn the inhabitants of
both islands. But the pirates could
not be held off indefinitely. In
1566, French freebooters managed
to invade Funchal, their reign of
terror lasting for 16 days. By the
time help arrived from the Portuguese mainland, all the churches
and the supplies of the great trading houses had been plundered.
When Portugal surrendered its independence to Spain for sixty years
(1580 – 1640), Madeira also came under Spanish rule. Both the island
and the mainland were thrust into the conflict between Spain and
England and were now plundered and pillaged by English pirates. In
1620, the English buccaneer John Ward launched an attack on Funchal, taking 1200 men, women and children captive and selling them
as slaves in Tunisia.

> **? DID YOU KNOW ...?**
>
> ■ One of the sweetest gifts ever offered in
> veneration of a pope came from Madeira: to
> thank Pope Leo X for ordaining his son as the
> first bishop of Madeira, the governor of the
> island sent him a replica model of St Peter's
> Basilica in Rome, made out of sugar.

English Presence

From 1660	English wine merchants settle
1807 – 1814	English occupation of Madeira
1852 / 1872	Mildew and phylloxera destroy the vines.
1891	Reid's Hotel is opened.

In 1660, Catharine of Braganza, daughter to João IV, married King **The English on**
Charles II of England. The marriage contract secured particular **Madeira**
rights for London with regard to Madeira – indeed, the island almost
exchanged hands as a dowry.
Before long, the first English merchants settled on Madeira. They
profited from trade privileges, especially with regard to Madeira
wine, which rapidly became the most important export commodity
of the island. A commercial treaty signed in 1703, leading to **Portugal's dependence on England** in the long run, saw Madeira's entire
wine production fall under English control.

Trade ships in the Bay of Funchal in the 19th century

Napoleonic Wars
During the Napoleonic Wars, English troops erected a stronghold on the island against France in 1801. When Napoleon annexed the Portuguese mainland in 1807, England declared its occupation of Madeira complete, but withdrew again in 1814. More than a few of the occupying officers and soldiers left the army and chose to remain on Madeira as merchants.

Economic downfall and renewed upturn
Mildew ruined a large part of the Madeiran vineyard in 1852; grape phylloxera brought in from America in 1872 proved equally devastating for a large proportion of the crop. It took years for grapes to grow again on more resilient vines. English vintners left the island and many impoverished Madeirans emigrated.

Others tried their luck at basketry, whilst new techniques of embroidery introduced by the Englishwoman Elizabeth Phelps led to a small-scale, yet consistent economic upturn. A further source of income, modest at first, was the emergence of tourism in the second half of the 19th century. The now world-famous Reid's Hotel opened its doors for the first time in 1891 (►Baedeker Special, p. 148); guests included royalty from all over Europe, some already crowned, some not. Among those who valued the healthy, rejuvenating qualities of the temperate climate was Empress Elisabeth (»Sissi«) of Austria.

20th Century

1914–1918	Portugal sides with England
1931	The »hunger revolution« is suppressed.
1933	Salazar's dictatorship begins.
1964	Madeira's airport is opened.
1974	The »Carnation Revolution« brings an end to the dictatorship.
1986	Portugal joins the EU.
2004	Madeira is European Region of the Year.

Portugal sided with England in the First World War. London enjoined the Portuguese government to seize all German ships anchored in Portuguese ports and hand them over to Great Britain. As a consequence, Germany dispatched submarines to Madeira, sinking the French warship *Surprise* off the coast of Funchal and opening fire on the town, where a number of buildings were destroyed. The population prayed for an end to the bombardment in a supplicatory procession, vowing to erect a statue of the Virgin Mary when the war ended – and the enemy fire ceased forthwith. The figure of the Virgin Mary was mounted above Monte in 1927, financed by donations from all over the world – even the Austrian Empress Zita is said to have contributed.

Successful supplicatory procession

In 1931, a revolt broke out on Madeira in a reaction to a decree issued by the government in Lisbon, giving mill owners the exclusive right to import flour. This led to a huge **increase in the price of bread**. Fearing for their livelihood, the islanders instigated the only general strike in the history of Madeira. On 4 April 1931 the »hunger uprising« spilled over into armed revolt, but on 28 April mainland troops arrived in Funchal and the rebels were forced to surrender after brief resistance.

General strike

From 1932, **António de Oliveira Salazar** (1889–1970) ruled the Portuguese motherland. His dictatorship was underpinned chiefly by the feared **secret police** PIDE. The constitution of 1933 established his authoritarian form of government, suppressing all opposition.
The Second World War left Madeira almost completely unscathed, Portugal remaining neutral. In May 1943, Lisbon severed diplomatic relations with Germany and subsequently allowed the British and Americans to set up military bases on the Azores.

Dictatorship

Regular flights by seaplane from southern England and Lisbon had been scheduled to Funchal since 1947. When the NATO airfield on Porto Santo was declared ready for use in 1960, visitors were able to

Increased tourism

land there and continue to Madeira by boat. To the east of Funchal, Santa Catarina Airport opened in 1964. This was followed by a **double-digit rate of increase** in visitor numbers.

Following the Salazar dictatorship (until 1968) and the six-year tenure of Salazar's confidant and successor Marcelo Caetano, the Movement of the Armed Forces (MFA) opposition group brought down the dictatorial regime in the largely bloodless »Carnation Revolution« in 1974. Amongst the parties formed were the radical FLAMA (Frente de Libertação do Arquipélago da Madeira) and MAIA (Movimento da Autonomia das Ilhas Atlánticas), who sought to achieve total independence from Portugal using tactics such as bomb attacks. Yet shortly before the parliamentary elections in 1976, the islands of the archipelago had been granted considerable self-governing rights as the Autonomous Region of Madeira. Hence, in 1978, 65% of the island's electorate voted for Dr. **Alberto João Cardoso Gonçalves Jardim** of the liberal-conservative party, the PSD (Partido Social Democrático), as regional president. A politician of the popular right, not without his share of controversy having also fallen under suspicion of corruption, he was re-elected for the last time in October 2004 with just 54% of the vote in a paltry 60% turnout. The government in Lisbon does supervise the Madeiran parliament and its government, but as far as internal affairs are concerned, Madeira retains a degree of **independence**, in financial policy, taxes and customs duties, for instance.

Bloodless revolution

Portugal became a member of the EU in 1986. The formation of the single European market in 1993 led to Madeira receiving EU funds, particularly for the improvement of the island's road network and the development of tourism. Since 2000, Santa Catarina Airport has benefited from an extended runway, built on concrete columns in the ocean. This enables wide-bodied aircraft to land on Madeira. In 2004, Madeira was voted European Region of the Year, an EU initiative to promote regional identity.

EU funding

← *EU support is vital for this type of cultivated terrain*

Arts and Culture

What does sugar have to do with art? How did Flemish masterpieces of the 15th and 16th centuries end up in Madeira, of all places? Manueline – what is it and where can it be found? Where did the azulejos come from? And what is a »brinquinho«?

Art History

As the economy and culture of Portugal blossomed under King Manuel I (1495–1521), Portuguese architecture found itself similarly inspired. The Manueline style was comparable in creative terms to the late Gothic and early Renaissance styles prevalent in Europe around the same time, yet possessed a distinct sense of originality and clear signs of Oriental or Indian influence too. The ascent of Portugal to the position of the world's leading naval power was also reflected in the nation's works of art and architecture. A notable characteristic of Manueline style is its fondness for decorative detail – not unlike the Plateresque style in Spain – often featuring **naturalistic elements** taken from marine life and seafaring, e.g. knotted rope, coiled hawsers, mussels or coral. One fine example of this rich ornamentation can be admired in a Manueline window in the Quinta das Cruzes garden in Funchal. Another, somewhat less ostentatious, is a small doorway arch at the Old Customs House (►p. 48 and Sights from A to Z, Funchal). Madeira cannot lay claim to anything in the Manueline style quite as grand as the Mosteiro dos Jerónimos at Belém on the Portuguese mainland. The island's provincial status and its distant location were hardly a tempting platform for ambitious architects or artists.

Manueline style

In contrast to the Portuguese mainland, architects on Madeira adopted elements of the Mudéjar style. Mudéjars were Arabs who lived in Portugal, reconquered by the Christians, from the 13th to the 15th century. Some church ceilings on Madeira were built in the Mudéjar style. A beautiful example of this work can be seen in Funchal Cathedral, whilst some smaller village churches also feature Mudéjar ceilings.

Mudéjar style

The 18th century saw many churches, hitherto fashioned in Manueline or Mudéjar style, decorated in Baroque splendour. There are countless examples of late Baroque, first and foremost altars adorned with gilded wood carvings (Talha Dourada). Where late Baroque meets earlier design, the interaction can be fascinating (as in the cathedral of Funchal, for example).

Baroque

In the 1970s, two works by the Brazilian architect **Oscar Niemeyer** were constructed on Madeira – a casino and, adjacent, a long hotel building. Niemeyer had found international fame on the strength of his designs for Brasília, the capital of Brazil, which was completely rebuilt in the latter half of the 1950s.

20th century

← *This enchanting azulejo fountain is one of the most beautiful on Madeira*

Painting: no independent developments

Whilst a relatively independent school of painting developed on the Portuguese mainland between the 15th and 18th centuries, painters born or living on Madeira drew their inspiration from the motherland, as evident primarily in the field of religious painting. No Madeiran artist enjoyed a reputation to rival such important Portuguese painters as Vasco Fernandes (known as Grão Vasco), Gregório Lopes or Cristóvão de Figueiredo. The prevalence of **Flemish paintings** in the churches and museums of Madeira can be traced back to the direct trading relations between Madeira and Flanders, which were in place from around 1472. Sugar from the island was such a prized commodity that some Madeiran merchants accepted paintings by famous artists in return.

Azulejos

Azulejos are **ceramic tiles**, imported from Spain since the beginning of the 16th century. The first imports were relief tiles crafted by Moorish artisans employing reds, greens, browns and blues in geometric patterns. Later, azulejo manufactories were established in Portugal itself (mainly in Lisbon, Porto and Coimbra), using different motifs. Moreover, they no longer manufactured reliefs, but flat tiles inspired by Italo-Flemish design. The fired terracotta tile was coated in a white tin-glaze and decorated with metal oxide paint. The azulejos made their way from the Portuguese mainland to the colonies and overseas territories.

Azulejo production reached a peak in the 17th century. Characteristic for this period are **carpet compositions** (tapetes) in blue, white and yellow with a wide variety of images. Such »carpets« covered every architectural space imaginable – altars and walls in churches, stairwells, fountains, benches, façades and the inside walls of elegant houses. They were also used as street signs. When the royal Portuguese court relocated to Brazil at the beginning of the 19th century and the mainland was rocked by civil war, azulejo manufacture wound down almost completely, recovering only around the mid-19th century. As in Brazil, tiles henceforth covered entire façades and inner walls of residential, commercial and civic buildings. Azulejo decoration experienced a resurgence at the turn of the 19th century and again at the end of the 20th century, with modern designs seen adorning numerous walls. Funchal's Museu Frederico de Freitas offers a valuable insight into the art form and its manifestations. Most of the azulejos now visible on Madeira are more recent, commonly mass-produced, examples. They are nevertheless most attractive to look at. Some of the island's churches still feature remarkable azulejo pictures of more historic origin. Almost unknown on the Portuguese mainland, Madeira is notably home to a number of **tiled church steeples**. The tiles on the steeple of Funchal Cathedral date back to

Azulejos on Madeira today ►

Mosaic paving art on the town hall square in Funchal, one of many examples on Madeira

the 16th century, making them some of the oldest azulejos on Madeira.

Pavement mosaics

As on the Portuguese mainland, many pavements and squares on Madeira are laid with mosaic stones in imaginative arrangements. Most common are black and white patterns, often featuring artistic motifs such as sailing ships or coats of arms. Funchal's Town Hall Square is completely paved with mosaic stones in a wave-like form. Pathways of dark basalt stone, a feature of the Canary Islands, can also be found on Madeira; the stones vary in shape and size and are arranged in geometric patterns.

Rooftop figures

»Remates de tecto« is the name given to the figures perched on roof-top corners, mostly seen on houses in the countryside. Doves are the most prevalent creatures, although a human face or a dog may also be spotted. The fired clay figures, made in the same way as the roofing tiles, are designed to protect those living under the roof by warding off evil spirits.

Costumes, Dance and Music

Traditional costumes

The costumes worn by Madeirans in years gone by have virtually disappeared from daily life, reappearing only on **festive occasions**. The

Although often played with tourists in mind, music is taken seriously

women wear knee-length pleated skirts in colourful stripes, a white blouse and decoratively knitted waistcoat under a kind of cape. The attire of the basket tobogganists of Monte consists of a straw hat with a black hatband, wide white trousers and shirt. Some elements of traditional dress can still be seen, usually in rural areas, such as **hats of sheep's wool** (»barrete de lã«). Goatskin **boots** with turned-down bootlegs (»botas«) and white or brown suits, worn with a red sash around the waist, are also a typical sight on festive occasions or holidays.

Dances Many dances present a stylized version of traditional agricultural labours. Religious celebrations, often spilling over into lively folk festivities, are a marvellous opportunity to see an array of traditional dances. The annual folklore festival in Santana, rich in authentic song and dance performance, is especially recommended.

Music Madeira's music is largely aligned with that of the Portuguese mainland. Scant evidence has survived of influence from other cultures, from slaves deported to the island, for instance. A video shown in the Museu Etnográfico in Ribeira Brava has captured singing with such a history. Perhaps the most typical form of folk music on Madeira is the so-called »**desfaio**« (also known as »despique«); no village fete is complete without it.

! *Baedeker* TIP

Music from Madeira

Portugal Canta 2 is the title of a CD showcasing, amongst others, the vocal talents of Sidónio da Silva and João Luís Mendoca with songs from Madeira.

Two singers relate the events of village and family life in rhyme, with little mishaps a source of great hilarity amongst the members of the audience. Instrumental accompaniment comes courtesy of the guitar-like »braguinha«, for example. Other folklore instruments commonly heard include the accordion, guitar, violin, flute, drums and a kind of ratchet (»reque-reque«), which probably originated in Africa. The **»brinquinho«** is a form of Turkish crescent. Its mechanism features miniature dolls, fastened to a wooden pole, its clappers and little bells creating a rhythm in much the same way as castanets. Brinquinhos can be purchased in many souvenir shops.

One very characteristic form of Portuguese music is **fado**. Fado concerts are staged on Madeira, but primarily with tourists in mind. The roots of fado are thought to lie in African or Brazilian folk music. A fado singer (fadista) is always accompanied by two guitars. The songs generally have a narrative quality and are often melancholy in character.

Handicrafts

Embroidery on the island can be traced back to the 16th century or thereabouts: Madeiran womenfolk were already highly acclaimed for their creative dexterity by this time. Until the mid-19th century, their efforts were almost exclusively for their own homes. In 1850, however, the foundations were laid for embroidery on an industrial scale: thanks to **Elizabeth (»Bella«) Phelps**, a dynamic member of an English wine merchant family, these exquisite works of artisanship made their way overseas, to England for example, where they caused a stir at the 1851 Great Exhibition in London. On the initiative of Elizabeth Phelps, numerous Madeiran families whose vineyards had been destroyed by mildew were able to build up a new livelihood. The golden age of embroidery – **white work** in particular – arrived in the early 20th century. The 1930s saw industrial needlework production step up, with copied patterns distributed to embroiderers living on the island.

Even today, more than half of the embroidered pieces are created in the home; the textiles are, however, prepared in the factory before home workers apply the finishing touches. Designs are often perforated in the linen by machine, the »máquina de picotar«. The **Instituto de Bordados, Tapeçaria e Artesanato da Madeira** (IBTAM, Institute for Embroidery, Tapestry and Handicrafts of Madeira), founded in 1978, strives to provide embroiderers with qualified training and see that they are paid fairly for their work. It issues a seal of quality and organizes a worldwide sales network.

The earliest documented record of Madeiran tapestries dates back to the year 1780. Various foreigners also got involved in the **needle-**

Embroidery, made in Madeira

point trade. Portraits, fantastic landscapes and paintings by the old masters are the most popular motifs.

The basket weavers of Madeira enjoy an excellent reputation, especially those in the small village of Camacha. Their raw material grows best of all in the damp valleys of the north coast. Basket-weaving is roughly as old as traditional embroidery. Twigs of osier, a cross between Salix alba and Salix fragilis, are used in weaving. Once they have been gathered, the twigs are stripped and boiled in large tubs, giving them their typical brown hue.

The basket weavers of Camacha

Basket-weaving prospered after 1945 as demand for wicker furniture and goods rose across Europe. Manufacturing costs rose dramatically in the 1970s, leading to a slump and stagnating revenue, but the latter part of the 20th century saw a renewed boom, principally due to an increase in visitors. Under the direction of the state institute for handicrafts, traditional weaving techniques have been revived and modern methods introduced for the gathering and treatment of osier rods. The local basket-weaving trade faces stiff competition from the cheaper markets of Eastern Europe and Asia. Unlike embroidery, there is no official seal of quality for basket-weaving, at least not yet.

> **! Baedeker TIP**
>
> **The finest Madeira embroidery**
> Not only is the Instituto de Bordados, Tapeçaria e Artesanato da Madeira (IBTAM) responsible for issuing a seal of quality for Madeiran embroidery, it also exhibits a splendid collection of craftworks, largely from the 19th century, in some of its rooms (opening hours: Mon – Fri 10am – 12.30pm and 2pm – 5.30pm).

← *Solid craftsmanship in Funchal*

Famous People

A handsome list of illustrious visitors reveals just how much at home the higher nobility felt on Madeira. Old photographs and bronze casts even document the presence of royalty.

John Blandy (1783 – 1855)

Born in Dorchester (England), John Blandy set foot on Madeira for the first time in 1807, as quartermaster of the British garrison. He liked the place so much that he settled here – having quit military service – four years later. Blandy acquired the house at Rua de São Francisco 8, where he founded his trading company, having immediate success with Madeira wine. »Blandy's Madeira Wine Company« developed into a trading house renowned throughout the whole of Europe, with thriving branches not only in England, but also in Lisbon and, later, on Gran Canaria. The foundation of Blandy's subsequent riches lay in his simple and astute practice of using incoming ships that carried coal or other cargo to Madeira as a means of shipping wine at favourable freight prices back to their home ports. Despite suffering a series of setbacks whilst at the helm, John Blandy's son Charles Ridpath (1812–1879) nevertheless managed to expand the company founded by his father. Looking beyond the wine trade, he began to import all kinds of goods, which his ships carried from England to Madeira. Charles Ridpath's own sons, for their part, made a name for themselves by instigating a public drinking water network in Funchal. Moreover, they published Madeira's first newspaper, the *Diário de Notícias,* which still exists today. In 1936 the Blandy family took over the prestigious Reid's Hotel, eventually selling it in the summer of 1996 to an international hotel chain. The Blandy family tomb can be found in the British cemetery in Funchal.

Wine merchant

Winston Churchill (1874 – 1965)

Of the many famous people attracted to Madeira by its mild climate and lush vegetation, Winston Churchill stands out. Son to the Conservative politician Lord Randolph Churchill, he was born on 30 November, 1874 in Blenheim Palace. Churchill first came to notice as a correspondent in the Boer War, and stopped on Madeira more than once while on his way to South Africa. The island inspired him to write a short story, *Mr. Keegan's Elopement,* set in the British community on Madeira at the end of the 19th century. Some 50 years later, in January 1950, Churchill returned to the island. Although his plan was to take a quiet holiday to recover from bad health without publicity and to prepare for the rigours of an expected election campaign, news of his arrival got out, and cheering crowds were waiting when he disem-

British politician

← *Elisabeth, the beautiful Empress of Austria, commemorated by a bronze statue on Madeira*

barked in Funchal and headed to Reid's Palace Hotel, accompanied by his wife Clementine, his daughter Diana, two secretaries and two Special Branch detectives. He fell in love with the fishing village of Câmara de Lobos, where a small panoramic terrace now reminds visitors of the spot where he painted the colourful scenes before him. When prime minister Attlee called elections earlier than expected, the Churchills were forced to cut short their stay on Madeira after just eleven days.

Elisabeth I (1837 – 1898)

Empress of Austria and Queen of Hungary

Elisabeth I was born on 24 December 1837 in Munich, the second daughter of Duke Maximilian Joseph. Her marriage to Emperor Franz Joseph I in 1854 was motivated by political expediency, as she became Empress of Austria and, two years later, Queen of Hungary. She bore Crown Prince Rudolph as well as three daughters – Sophie, Gisela and Marie Valerie. Elisabeth I, known affectionately to the people as »Sissi«, was exceedingly well-educated, fluent in several languages, had a keen interest in music and sport, yet was quite probably a manic-depressive. Never at ease with the strict etiquette of courtly life, she drifted further and further into psychological isolation, an outsider at the imperial court. Restless journeys increasingly characterized her life. One of them brought her to Madeira in 1860. She arrived in a sickly condition, and some doctors even suspected consumption. For close to six months, she resided in the Quinta das Angústias, where today, the official residence of the regional government, Quinta Vigia, now stands. The Atlantic island's temperate climate improved her state of health, but her inner disquiet persisted. She left Madeira on 28 April 1861, ultimately returning to the imperial court in Vienna. On 10 September 1898, Elisabeth I was murdered in Geneva by the Italian anarchist Luigi Luccheni. Her life gave rise to numerous romantic novels and many films besides, which generally overlooked her intelligence and education to focus on her beauty, with which she herself was obsessed. Playing the lead in the »Sissi films« made a worldwide star of Romy Schneider.

Henry the Navigator (1394 – 1460)

Discoverer

Although Henry (Portuguese: Henrique), the third son of the Portuguese King João I, never set sail on any lengthy seafaring expedition, history would bestow the title of »the Navigator« upon him (in Portuguese: o Navegador). Born on 4 March 1394, the young Infante, as Portuguese and Spanish princes were known, owed his fame to the conquest of Ceuta in the year 1415. As a mark of his appreciation, the king made him Duke of Viseu and handed him control of the defences and administration of the conquered town in North Africa. Old nautical charts, manuscripts and stories told by returning mariners awakened the young prince's interest in seafaring. Appointed Grand Master of the Order of Christ in 1418, the financial riches of this successor of the dissolved Knights Templar were now at his disposal. This enabled him to convert his seafaring dreams into reality. At the southwestern tip of Portugal, in Sagres, he founded a kind of research centre, where the newest discoveries in navigation, astronomy and the like were exchanged and examined in depth. In addition, a completely new type of ship was constructed, the caravel. In terms of manoeuvrability and seaworthiness, it was far superior to any sailing ships seen thus far. Over the next few years, Henry financed one voyage of discovery after another. First of all, the Madeira Islands were discovered, or rather, rediscovered and colonized by 1423 (in the year 1433, Prince Henry was granted tenure of the archipelago by King Duarte). Next in his sights

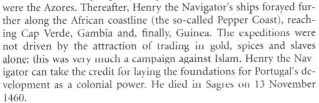

were the Azores. Thereafter, Henry the Navigator's ships forayed further along the African coastline (the so-called Pepper Coast), reaching Cap Verde, Gambia and, finally, Guinea. The expeditions were not driven by the attraction of trading in gold, spices and slaves alone; this was very much a campaign against Islam. Henry the Navigator can take the credit for laying the foundations for Portugal's development as a colonial power. He died in Sagres on 13 November 1460.

Karl I (1888 – 1922)

Karl I, a great-nephew of Emperor Franz Joseph I, was born on 17 August 1887 in Persenbeug (Lower Austria). As his uncle Franz Ferdinand, the heir to the throne, was assassinated on 28 June 1914 in Sarajevo, he succeeded Franz Joseph as Emperor of Austria and King of Hungary on 21 December 1916. His unfortunate reign lasted just two years, marking the end of the era of the Habsburg dynasty and coinciding with the end of the First World War; inside Austria, he fell short of effecting any meaningful reforms. Not least through the pressure of the Russian Revolution of 1917, he renounced participation in government in Austria and Hungary, without officially abdicating. Having twice failed to reclaim the throne in Hungary, he was exiled to Madeira and died here, the last Habsburg emperor, of respiratory failure on 1 April 1922. The sarcophagus containing the mortal remains of Karl I has remained on the island to this day in Monte, in the Church of Our Lady of Monte (Nossa Senhora do Monte). His beatification took place in 2004.

Emperor of Austria and King of Hungary

Christopher Columbus (1451–1506)

Seafarer and explorer Christopher Columbus is thought to have been born in Genoa. Aged 25, he came to Lisbon and soon became interested in the western sea route to India, which had been talked about since ancient times. His idea of launching an expedition to explore this seaway fell on deaf ears at the royal court of Portugal, so Columbus initially turned his attention to maritime trade. In 1478, he paid his first visit to Madeira to buy sugar for a Genoese businessman living in Lisbon. Here, he

made the acquaintance of Filipa Moniz – daughter of Bartolomeu Perestrelo, the first Portuguese governor of the neighbouring island of Porto Santo – and a year later they married. As a result, Columbus gained access to the higher echelons of Portuguese society, probably living on Porto Santo from 1479 to 1484, which is quite likely where he developed his plans for a western expedition. When the Junta dos Matemáticos in Lisbon conclusively rejected his request for financial support, Columbus headed for Spain. He left the harbour of Palos in 1492 with three ships and discovered the Bahamas island of Guanahaní (known today as San Salvador) three months later. It was not the Indian continent he had expected to find, but the Americas. Nevertheless, until his death on 20 May 1506 in Valladolid, Spain, Columbus remained convinced that he had discovered the western sea route to India. Since 1899 his final resting place has been in Seville, although it is not certain that his remains are really contained in the sarcophagus. On Porto Santo, the Casa de Colombo (Columbus House) is now a museum. Columbus is said to have lived here, although there is no firm historical evidence to substantiate this.

Cristiano Ronaldo (born 1985)

Football player Cristiano Ronaldo dos Santos Aveiro was born in the Santo António district of Funchal, the youngest of four children. His father, a gardener, chose the name Ronaldo in honour of his favourite actor, Ronald Reagan. Cristiano Ronaldo played for the youth teams of the Madeiran football clubs Adorinha and Nacional before moving to the Portuguese mainland to play for Sporting Lisbon in 1997. In 2003 he was signed by Manchester United, where he was given the no. 7 shirt that had been worn by George Best and David Beckham, and was a member of teams that won the English Premier League three times and the Champions League once, in 2008. He transferred to Real Madrid in 2009 for the highest fee ever paid for a footballer, £80 million. He has played as a winger and forward for the Portuguese national team, taking part in the FIFA World Cup competitions in 2006 and 2010, and scoring 25 goals in 79 international matches between 2003 and 2010.

Manuel I (1469 – 1521)

King of Portugal

Visitors to the island of Madeira are offered frequent reminders of the legacy of King Manuel I, not least in the form of the architectural style to which he lent his name. It features Gothic, early Renaissance and Indo-Oriental elements. Manuel was born in 1469 as the youngest son of the Infante Fernando. When the heir to the throne was killed in a riding accident, Manuel was proclaimed king on 27 October 1495 in Alcácer do Sal. Manuel I engineered close relations to Spain through his three marriages. His first queen, in 1497, was Isabella of Asturias, the widow of the Infante Afonso. After her death, he married her sister, Maria of Aragon, who gave birth to the future King João III. Eleanor of Habsburg, although initially intended to be his own son's bride, would be his third and final wife. Under Manuel I's rule, royal power was strengthened at the expense of the nobility, public administration was centralized and tax and customs laws rationalized. More than anything, however, his reign is associated with voyages of discovery, which the monarch patronized primarily out of commercial interest. Vasco da Gama was thus commissioned to follow the sea route to India and Pedro Álvares Cabral set sail for Brazil. Lisbon advanced to the status of Europe's leading trade port, and Manuel was nicknamed »the Fortunate« or »the Great«. The influx of riches was also manifested in architectural development, but Portugal's golden age would not last long: by the time of Manuel I's death in 1521, its zenith had already passed.

Practicalities

WHAT IS IN A PONCHA? WHERE IS THE NICEST PLACE TO GO SWIMMING? AND HOW DO YOU GET YOUR WICKER CHAIR HOME? FIND OUT HERE – BEFORE YOUR HOLIDAY, IDEALLY!

Accommodation

Accommodation for every pocket Madeira offers a wide selection of hotels, guesthouses and somewhat more unusual accommodation in so-called »quintas«. It is known for its many large, **upmarket hotels** – approximately 17% of all accommodation on the island is in 5-star hotels, and a quarter of the hotels are in the 4-star bracket. Package deals tend to be more affordable. Booking individually may well prove more expensive.

Most of the big hotels are in Funchal or dotted around the outskirts of the capital. To the west of the centre, along the Estrada Monumental, parallel to the coast, a sprawling and still growing **hotel zone** has arisen with a high-quality infrastructure for tourists. The hotels, some of them around 4km/2.5mi outside Funchal, usually run their own shuttle bus service to the town centre, whilst several municipal bus routes follow the Estrada Monumental on their way into town.

Outside Funchal In the outlying villages, smaller houses of more individual character can be found, as well as a few fairly basic guesthouses (pensão), offering sound, reasonably priced accommodation. In terms of price and

Madeira makes it possible: an overnight stay amidst a sea of blossoms

comfort, a **residencial** is comparable to a good guesthouse or small hotel, whilst an **estalagem** is a little more comfortable. Built in the 19th century, **quintas** are, as a rule, stylishly appointed estates, some of which can be found in Funchal, though they are more commonly located in the countryside. They often have just a few rooms available for rent, hence their predominantly familial atmosphere. Further details from the ► tourist information centres. **Private accommodation** (quartos) is a rarity on Madeira. The best idea is to enquire at the tourist information offices on the island. A number of hotels and guesthouses provide self-catering rooms with a kitchen.

There are no campsites on Madeira at present: a site at Porto Moniz has fallen victim to modernization measures, although a replacement is in the planning stages. There is a campsite on Porto Santo, open all year round.

Advance booking is recommended for the **high season** (► When to Go). The price of a double room can vary considerably from season to season, with particularly sharp rises possible around Christmas and New Year.

Booking and prices

Arrival · Before the Journey

Getting There

There are regular air connections between mainland Europe and Madeira. The Portuguese airline TAP has daily **scheduled flights** from London to Madeira: from Gatwick direct to Funchal, and from Heathrow to Funchal via Lisbon. TAP also flies from Lisbon to Porto Santo. In addition, **charter flights** to Madeira are available from a number of British and Irish airports, e.g. Thomson Air from Birmingham, East Midland, Exeter, Glasgow and London Gatwick. Among operators and **budget flights**, Jet2com flies direct from Leeds and Manchester to Funchal, easyjet direct from Bristol and London Stansted and Gatwick to Funchal. The flight time from London to Madeira is approximately three and a half hours. Porto Santo can be reached from Madeira; this flight takes around 15 minutes.

By air

If you have lots of time and a generous budget, there are two alternatives to flying: the five-day voyage on a cargo ship from Felixstowe to the Madeiran port of Caniçal, returning via the Canary Islands and Cadiz (Strand Voyages of London, tel. 020 7921 4340, www.strand-travelltd.co.uk), or the 27-hour train journey from London through France and Spain to the Algarve (book through Spanish Rail, tel. 020 7725 7063, www.spanish-rail.co.uk), followed by the 22-hour crossing on the weekly car ferry from Portimao to Madeira (Naviera Armas, tel. 00 351 265 546 300, www.navieraarmas.com).

GETTING THERE

AIRLINES

► **TAP – Air Portugal**
In London
Tel. 08 45 601 09 32, ticket desk at
22 Chapter St., London SW1

On Madeira:
Tel. 291 239 248 (Funchal airport)
Tel. 707 205 700 (Porto Santo)
www.tap.pt

► **easyjet**
Tel. 09 05 821 09 05
www.easyjet.com

► **Jet2**
Tel. 08 71 226 17 37
www.jet2.com

MADEIRA AIRPORT

► **Location**
approx. 18 km/11 mi east of
Funchal

► **Taxi to Funchal**
Journey time approx. 30 minutes,
costs between 20 and 30 €,
according to destination.

► **Airport bus**
Every hour or every two hours to
Funchal and hotel area.

► **Package holiday customers**
are generally collected by a hotel
bus.

Cruise ships   Madeira is a popular destination for cruise ships all year round, although most of them only dock at Funchal Harbour for one or two days.

Immigration and Customs Regulations

Travel documents   Travellers from Europe require a valid passport or national identity card. Children under the age of 16 must be in possession of a child's travel document (with photo if aged 10 or above) or be registered on a parent's passport.

Car papers   A national driving licence usually suffices to rent a vehicle. This should be carried at all times, together with vehicle registration documents and green card (International Motor Insurance Certificate).

Pets   Those wishing to take their pets with them (dogs, cats) to Madeira will need an **EU Pet Passport**, which can be obtained from a vet, including proof of a valid rabies vaccination, which must be at least thirty days old but not older than 12 months.

Customs regulations   The states of the European Union form a common economic area, the **European Single Market**, in which the movement of goods for private use is largely exempt from duty. There are certain allowances which travellers from other European countries need to be aware of when arriving in Portugal and Madeira (e.g. a maximum of 800 cigarettes, 10 litre of spirits and 90 litres of wine for visitors over 17 years of age).

For travellers from outside the EU, the following duty-free quantities apply: 200 cigarettes or 100 cigarillos or 50 cigars or 250g of tobacco; also 2 litres of wine and 2 litres of sparkling wine or 1 litre of spirits with an alcohol content of more than 22% vol.; 500g of coffee or 200g of coffee extracts, 100g of tea or 40g of tea extract, 50ml of perfume or 0.25 litres of eau de toilette. Gifts up to a value of €175 are also duty-free.

> ! **Baedeker TIP**
>
> **Copies**
>
> It is advisable to make copies of travel documents and keep them at the hotel, as this will make it easier to secure duplicate papers in the event of the originals being lost.

Travel Insurance

Medical care on holiday is provided if a **European Health Insurance Card** (European Health Insurance Card, EHIC) is presented to the doctor. This card has now replaced the previous health insurance forms. Even with the card, a portion of the costs of treatment or medicines must, in many cases, be paid for by the patient. On production of the receipts, the outlay will be reimbursed on returning home – although not for every treatment.

Public health insurance

As the patient often has to pay a share of the costs for medical treatment and medicines, and return transport, if necessary, is not covered by public health insurance, an additional private health insurance policy is recommended.

Private health insurance

Beaches

Madeira cannot claim to be the greatest island for bathing. Its few beaches are generally pebbly rather than sandy. Bathing shoes or sandals and a thick blanket or towel come in very handy on the rough stones. Nevertheless, along the coast, Madeira does have a number of man-made bathing resorts and smaller swimming complexes or lidos known as »Complexo Balnear« or »Balneário«. Furthermore, almost every hotel on Madeira has its own swimming pool. Porto Santo, on the other hand, has sand aplenty: the 9km/5.5mi of beach at Campo de Baixo are popular during the holiday season and at weekends for Madeiran families, but it is still possible to find a quiet spot.

> **? DID YOU KNOW …?**
>
> ■ 40,000 cubic metres/1.4 million cubic feet of desert sand were shipped by container from Morocco to create the artificial sandy beach at Calheta.

Pebble Beaches and Bathing Resorts on Madeira

Stony and pebbly beaches, rough in places, can be found at **Ribeira Brava and Ponta do Sol**, for example. At **Madalena do Mar** there are two places to go swimming, one before and one after the tunnel. **Fajã dos Padres** comprises a handful of houses and a simple restaurant on a pebble beach with concrete flagstones. Access is by boat or the elevator which descends from the top of the Cabo Girão. There are also coarse pebble beaches to the east, in **Santa Cruz and Machico**. At the western edge of **Funchal** lies Praia Formosa, its atmosphere somewhat tarnished by the oil tanks close by. In some places, such as **Calheta**, breakwaters divide bathing areas from the open sea, their calmer waters making swimming more manageable. **Faial** boasts an artificial lagoon, offering protection from the more powerful waves.

i **The best beaches**

- Lava swimming pools in Porto Moniz
- Porto Santo sandy beach
- Santa Cruz water park
- Complexo Balnear da Ponta Gorda in Funchal

Sandy beaches The only natural sandy beach with a fair covering of sand is the »Prainha« – literally, the little beach – between Caniçal and the Ponta de São Lourenço peninsula. Madeira's second sandy beach, in Calheta, was artificially landscaped.

Sea Bathing Pools and Swimming Pools

An excellent alternative comes in the form of naturally occurring **lava swimming pools**. They have the great advantage of offering respite from the full force of incoming waves. Bathing shoes with non-slip soles are recommended. Two particularly charming lava swimming pools can be found in **Porto Moniz**, for instance. The newer of the two is a regular swimming pool with ample space to lie down, plus toilets and restaurant. The other is a lava landscape with sectioned-off pools.

Man-made swimming pools Smaller, artificial pools, into which tidal seawater flows, can be found in **Seixal, Ponta Delgada and Porto da Cruz**. Waves splash into these basins at high tide, whilst at low tide, the water is more placid and swimming a real pleasure. There is usually a nominal admission charge, which includes the use of changing facilities and toilets. The **Caniço de Baixo** tourism centre has two beautiful seawater swimming pools at Rocamar and Galomar. The sea pools of **Santa Cruz** and **Ribeira Brava** are also frequented by local Madeirans. No less popular are the new Piscinas das Salinas in **Câmara do Lobos** and the bathing complex in Caniçal.

Not the most comfortable beach to sit and walk on, but the water is splendid

Virtually every Funchal hotel has its own swimming pool, and some even have their own small lava pools. There are also several good public swimming baths with man-made pools and bathing spots in the sea, or seawater basins. East of the Forte de São Tiago lies the Barreirinha complex. The Complexo Balnear do Lido in the hotel zone features, amongst other things, an Olympic-size pool, 50 metres/55yd in length. Further west lie the Clube Naval and the Complexo Balnear das Poças do Governador. The most modern of all is the Complexo Balnear da Ponta Gorda, with several pools and a seawater basin.

Children

Madeira has much to offer families with children: **easy levada trails** leading through interesting scenery – across plateaus, through gorges, past waterfalls – are a great experience for older children. A variety of **seawater swimming pools** provide lots of fun on Madeira, particularly the larger ones at Porto Moniz and the Complexo Balnear (lido) and Complexo Balnear da Ponta Gorda in Funchal, which have children's pools. Most hotels have swimming facilities, often with a children's pool. An alternative is the long, sandy beach of Porto Santo, close by. Younger and older children will be thrilled by a **voyage on the *Santa Maria***, a replica of the ship on which Christo-

Fun for all ages

pher Columbus sailed when he discovered America. The expedition commences in Funchal harbour and steers a course along the west coast (►Baedeker Tip, p. 65).

A sightseeing programme for children can include the **bird park** in the Botanical Gardens, the **caves of São Vicente** or a **cable car ride** from Funchal up to Monte. More daring visitors can take to the skies with a balloon moored in the harbour of Funchal (►Baedeker Tip, p. 136). Children keen on technology will find plenty to do in the **Museu da Electricidade** in Funchal: a host of levers and switches can be operated to demonstrate different phenomena associated with electricity. Other popular attractions are the **Whale Museum** in Caniçal, the **Ethnographic Museum** in Ribeira Brava and the **Centro de Ciência Viva** and **Aquarium** in Porto Moniz. Many hotels, moreover, offer special activities for children in the holiday period.

Electricity

On Madeira the mains supply is **220 volts, 50 hertz**. Adaptors can be obtained at hotel receptions or in the shops in Funchal.

Emergency

USEFUL EMERGENCY NUMBERS

EMERGENCY NUMBERS

► **Tel. 112**
Police, fire brigade, ambulance, doctor (calls not charged)

MISCELLANEOUS

► **Coastguard**
Tel. 291 230 112

► **Breakdown service**
Tel. 800 290 290

Etiquette and Customs

What to wear   As in other southern countries, appropriate clothing is an important consideration. That applies **not only to restaurants in the evening** but also to a shopping or sightseeing trip. Scant leisure clothing is heavily frowned upon for church visits. Men should never be seen bare-chested except on the beach. Women can only go topless at the hotel pool, not on the beach or in public swimming baths.

Generally, it is not necessary to wait to be seated. The restaurant or
bar bill should not be split: the musketeer motto **»one for all«** is the
norm. Guests can, of course, choose to divide the bill amongst themselves afterwards, buy the next round or pay for the next dinner on
the next restaurant meal. This is how to pay: the waiter brings the
bill on a small plate. Once he has left the table, place a credit card or
the cash on the plate with the bill. Soon enough, the waiter will collect the plate and bring it back with the change. Leave a reasonable
tip on the plate. The waiter will collect it when the guests have left.

In restaurants

The Madeirans make a great effort to communicate with their guests
in English. However, a few words **of Portuguese** such as »bom dia«
(»good morning«) or perhaps to book a room, or order food in a
restaurant will certainly be welcomed by the locals as a gesture of
politeness to the host country.

Bom dia

Excursions

Hiring a car is a good way of getting to know Madeira, all the more
so since the road network has been improved with new highways
and tunnels. The older narrow, winding roads – the ones that are left
– are more picturesque by far, though a considerably slower means
of seeing the island (►Tours).
Buses reach all places on Madeira, some of them only scheduled
once a day, however. Reconnoitring the island by bus thus requires
meticulous planning (►transport).

Personal itinerary

A good number of travel agencies and tour operators in Funchal spe-
cialize in half-day or full-day tours of the island with tour guides
who speak English. Organized hikes, many following the levada
trails, are also offered by many tourist companies on the island.
These are an excellent option for
less experienced hikers, as sign-
posts are not particularly common.

Guided tours of the island, hikes

Boat trips can be booked directly
at the Funchal Marina information
and ticket booth. The Albatroz Or-
ganization offers half-day, or shorter, sailing trips on their *Albatroz*
yacht (parties of up to 20). Passen-
gers on board the *Katherine B.*,
captained by expert fisherman Peter Bristow, can look forward to
seeing dolphins and, with a little

> **!** *Baedeker* TIP
>
> **Sailing trip on the Santa Maria**
>
> In a wharf at Câmara de Lobos, a virtually true-
> to-scale replica of the ship with which Columbus
> sailed to the Americas has been built. It is
> possible to take a trip along the south coast of
> Madeira on this beautiful wooden ship. Details
> from: Santa Maria de Colombo, Actividades
> Marítimo-Turísticas, Lda Marina do Funchal;
> tel. / fax 291 220 327.

luck, whales. More information available from the tourism office. Traditional fishing methods are still followed on the *Ribeira Brava*, an old, restored fishing boat moored at Lugar de Baixo, to the west of Ribeira Brava. Further details regarding trips can be obtained by calling Claudia Gomes, tel. 291 771 582, lobosonda@sapo.pt.

To Porto Santo   The ferry crossing to Porto Santo (return trip approx. 50€) takes around two hours. A new ship has only recently come into service. Further information can be obtained in Rua da Praia, Funchal, tel. 291 210 300, and on the island of Porto Santo itself in Rua de Estévão Alencastre, tel. 291 982 543.

Festivals · Holidays · Events

As well as public holidays, there are also local Madeiran holidays with religious and traditional backgrounds. Up-to-date listings of festivals and holidays can be obtained in tourist information centres (►Information). Some hotels and restaurants stage regular displays of Madeiran folklore. In addition to public holidays, a number of lo- **Traditional events** cal religious and traditional holidays are celebrated on Madeira. Tourist information offices (information) will be able to supply up-to-date details. Some hotels and restaurants host regular Madeiran folklore events.

Music is part of the island life

● HOLIDAYS and FESTIVALS

PUBLIC HOLIDAYS

1 January
February/March: Shrove Tuesday, Ash Wednesday
March/April: Good Friday
25 April: Freedom Day; national holiday to commemorate the Carnation Revolution of 25 April 1974
1 May: Labour Day
May/June: Corpus Christi
10 June: Dia de Portugal or Camões Day; national holiday in remembrance of Portuguese poet Luis de Camões who died on 10 June 1580
1 July: Madeira Day of Discovery
15 August: Assumption of the Virgin
5 October: Republic Day; national holiday on the anniversary of the declaration of the Portuguese Republic on 5 October 1910
1 November: All Saints Day
1 December: National holiday to commemorate Portuguese Independence from Spain, 1 December 1640
8 December: Feast of the Immaculate Conception
25 and 26 December: Christmas

FEBRUARY/MARCH

► **Carnival**
For four days in a row, Madeirans celebrate carnival, the highlight being an organized procession through Funchal on the Saturday before Ash Wednesday. Another procession follows on Shrove Tuesday.

Flower children at the »Festa das Flores«

APRIL/MAY

▶ San Remo Festival of Flowers

The wonderful Festival of Flowers heralds the beginning of spring and is one of the most important events on the Madeiran calendar. On no account should the Funchal procession, featuring groups from all over the island, be missed. The whole of Funchal is decorated with a carpet of flowers.

JUNE

▶ Festival do Atlântico

This classical music festival attracts famous singers and orchestras from all over the world. Concerts are staged in churches, palaces, gardens and the municipal theatre of Funchal.

▶ São Pedro Festival

Colourful boat procession in Ribeira Brava, in honour of the patron saint of fishermen.

JULY

▶ 24 Horas de Bailar

24 hours of folklore in Santana with a wealth of music played on traditional instruments, singing and dancing – a treat not only for fans of folklore.

AUGUST

▶ Madeira Wine Rally

The Madeira Wine Rally takes place on the first weekend of August, as it has done since 1959, counting towards the European Rally Championship. The race covers the entire island – a very special challenge.

▶ Assumption of the Virgin

Spectacular procession and a grand festival in honour of Nossa Senhora do Monte in the mountain village of Monte.

SEPTEMBER

▶ Madeira Wine Festival

Rousing festival held at the beginning of the grape harvest in mid-September. The celebrations in Estreito de Câmara de Lobos are enthralling. Funchal also hosts Madeiran folklore events and wine tastings.

▶ Apple Festival

Apple harvest festival featuring homemade products in Ponta do Pargo. Other fruit and vegetables join the apple-based produce on sale.

▶ Christopher Columbus Week

Porto Santo stages a full week of events in honour of Christopher Columbus.

▶ Boat procession

Festa da Nossa Senhora da Piedade: boat procession in Caniçal, in which a statue of the Virgin Mary is carried on the water.

OCTOBER

▶ Apple festival in Camacha.

NOVEMBER

▶ Chestnut festival in Curral das Freiras.

DECEMBER

▶ Christmas

Funchal illuminations leading up to Christmas. Midnight mass in Funchal Cathedral is a highlight.

▶ New Year's Eve / New Year

Huge firework display in Funchal.

Food and Drink

Madeiran cookery is **heavily influenced by Portuguese cuisine**, which is characterized by hearty, down-to-earth fare rather than culinary experiments. If there is a basic principle underlying Portuguese cooking, it is the ability to make the very best out of the local farm produce available.

Down-to-earth cuisine

As in other southern countries, **breakfast** is a fairly simple meal. Only the larger tourist hotels offer a breakfast buffet with sausage, cheese, boiled or fried eggs and fruit. Guests who take breakfast in a café – as many Madeirans do – can order buttered toast (torrada), toast with ham and cheese (tosta mista) or a bread roll with cheese (sanduíche de queijo) or ham (sanduíche de fiambre).

Meals

Greater importance is accorded to **lunch and dinner**, which usually consist of two to three courses: a starter (entrada), main course – invariably meat or fish with potatoes or chips – and dessert (sobremesa), with home-made puddings, fruits or ice cream. **Appetizers** such as bread, butter, olives, cheese and paté, charged separately, are commonly brought to the table. Once in a while, expensive seafood may also be placed before diners without having been ordered. If sampled, this will also be charged for, but it is no problem to leave it untouched.

> ### *i* Specialities of the island
>
> - Espetada: chunks of meat on a laurel-twig kebab
> - Espada: scabbard fish with banana
> - Bolo de mel: honey cake
> - Aguardente: sugar-cane spirit

Delicious local dishes include »pão caseiro«, also known as »bolo de caco«, a kind of sweet potato bread that is baked to a traditional recipe in a stone oven. In the countryside, these are sold as flat cakes from roadside stalls, ideal fare for any journey.

A coffee in between times is as popular on Madeira as it is in Portugal. For Madeirans any time is right for this inexpensive treat. They stand at the counter for a quick coffee or meet for a chat over »bica« (espresso), »café com leite« (coffee with milk), »meia de leite« (with slightly less milk) or »galão« (milky coffee in a glass). There are plenty of simple cafés and pastelarias offering tasty little cakes, along with a number of bars serving home-made fare at reasonable prices. At the heart of Funchal, between the seafront and the cathedral, a number of large cafés and restaurants with tables outside are dotted about the promenade.

Time for coffee

Restaurants usually open from noon until 3pm and again from 6pm or 7pm. Dinner is normally served until 10pm. **Reservations** are generally advisable in the more upmarket restaurants and for larger parties.

Meal times

THE OLDER, THE BETTER

Nowhere else in the world is wine treated as it is on Madeira. And any wine connoisseur would shake his head, were it not for the exceptional taste of Sercial, Verdelho or Malvasia.

Yet it was a chance occurrence that set the ball rolling: Madeira wine pressed from imported grape varieties had a slightly tart taste which took some getting used to. The sailors who docked at Madeira to stock up on wine before embarking on their voyages of discovery reported a remarkable transformation in the flavour when the barrels were exposed to tropical heat. And once they had added a modicum of brandy to halt the fermentation process, the typical character of Madeira wine was complete.

Winemaking

In principle, winemaking on Madeira is the same today as it was 450 years ago. Perhaps the main difference is that the wine is no longer sent across the oceans to the tropics, but is heated locally to a temperature of 50°C/122°F. The solera process is used, with rows of barrels filled with wine according to quality and wines of similar character placed next to each other. From the lowest row of barrels containing the oldest wine, a certain amount is extracted and refilled with the same amount from the row of barrels immediately above. This process is repeated up to the top row, thus ensuring that a measure of newer wine is added to each older barrel. Only after a further stage of maturation is the wine ready to drink and filled into the distinctive bottles. Undated bottles tend to contain three-year-old wine. Restaurants and bars usually serve five-year-old wine; far more expensive, and accordingly far more refined, are the ten or fifteen-year-old varieties.

From dry to sweet

The most common varieties of grape are Sercial, Verdelho, Bual and Malmsey. This sequence also represents the

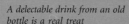
A delectable drink from an old bottle is a real treat

order of the wines in terms of increasing sweetness and full-bodied character. It is not, however, the grape that determines the degree of sweetness, but the quantity of added brandy and the timing of its addition. The driest, Sercial, is harvested as late as November and is particularly good as an aperitif. Malmsey, or Malvasia, is the sweetest. It is characterized by a certain acerbity and is thus seen as a suitable dessert wine. Verdelho is equally good for both purposes, whilst Bual is generally served as a dessert wine.

Storage

Madeira wine can be stored indefinitely. Some varieties still exude full-bodied freshness after a hundred years and more, although the price for such wine can be prohibitive. Whilst other wines are best stored horizontally, Madeira is better left standing upright: it does not need to absorb any more oxygen through the cork. Once opened, however, it should be drunk fairly quickly. Which should not present a problem to connoisseurs.

Madeira recipes

Madeira can be enjoyed on its own, but it can also be used as the basis for an exquisite sauce: take 0.5l/1 pint of meat stock, heat on a low flame until a third has boiled away (beat constantly with a whisk), then add four tablespoons of Madeira (Bual). Season with salt and pepper and serve immediately. It is the perfect accompaniment to veal.

The following recipe is also worth considering: mix thoroughly 6 cl/2 fl.oz of Madeira (any variety), 2 bar spoons of sugar syrup and one egg yolk in a shaker and serve in a long glass, garnished with grated nutmeg. This interesting blend is an afternoon tipple known as Madeira Flip.

Typical Regional Dishes

Soups

Tomato soup is a typical Madeira dish, with the addition of onions and – shortly before it is served – an egg. Another soup is the famous »caldo verde« with finely minced kale, savoy cabbage or chard. The broth can be clear or thick. Traditional Madeiran soups include sopa de trigo (from wheat), açorda (a clear broth with egg, garlic and bread) and sopa de agrumes, a watercress-based soup.

The Madeirans eat little pork or beef, but the meats can, of course, be found on restaurant menus. One typical speciality is **espetada da Madeira**, a laurel-twig meat kebab, barbecued over an open fire. Escalope and steak (bife) prepared in different ways, such as a typical Portuguese beefsteak (bife à portuguesa), are also commonly served. Grilled chicken (frango assado) is a cheap and popular dish.

Fish dishes

Fish dishes of many varieties, along with other sea creatures like »caramujos« (periwinkles), »caracóis« (snails) and »lapas« (limpets) are usually available on Madeira in fresh supply. An absolute Madeiran speciality is »espada preta« or simply »**espada**« (scabbard fish). Some restaurants serve the black, scaleless espada with a banana, in keeping with tradition. Other fish dishes worthy of mention are »atum« (tuna) and »bacalhau« (dried cod), customarily served with onions, garlic, olives and potatoes. Further items on the menu include »pargo« (red snapper), »espadarte« (swordfish), »garoupa« (grouper), »dourada« (sea bream) and sometimes »bodião« (wrasse). A delectable combination of seafood with rice, a kind of paella, is known as »arroz de marisco«.

Main courses are normally served with rice, potatoes or French fries. Other **side dishes** are uncommon in traditional Portuguese cuisine. It is often worth ordering an extra salad, at least, which will often arrive without dressing. Restaurants more accustomed to dealing with tourists are likely to include salad and perhaps vegetables with the main course.

The famous meat skewer: »Espetada da Madeira«

Baedeker TIP

The aroma of anona

The anona, or cherimoya, resembling a round, green fir cone, has a mouth-watering aroma. It can also be left to ripen for several days.

Dessert lovers should try »leite creme«, a lightly caramelized pudding made from sugar, egg and milk, or »arroz doce«, a rice pudding made with egg and sprinkled with cinnamon. Other desserts frequently seen on the menu are »pudim flan«, a kind of caramel pudding, and »pudim de maracuja« – passion fruit pudding. Or simply »bolo« (cakes) and »fruta(s)« – fresh fruits. Madeiran honey cake, »**bolo de mel**«, is a local speciality, also sold as a souvenir item. »Bolo de nata« or »pastel de nata« is a small, round custard tart made with flaky pastry.

Desserts and small cakes

Fruits are extremely popular on Madeira. The variety of mango cultivated on Madeira (Mangifera indica) is quite small, yellow and fibrous, but tastes wonderful. The long cones of the **philodendron** (Monstera deliciosa) which grow in the wild, as well as in gardens and parks, have a delicate, sweet taste when they are fully ripened. Passion fruit or maracuja have striking blossoms, and their fruits are used to make juice or eaten as dessert.

Drinks

Wine is still the traditional table drink on Madeira; most of the wines, however, come from the Portuguese mainland. A speciality is »**vinho verde**«, a light, acidic wine from northern Portugal, harvested early and only fermented for a short period. Fermentation continues in the bottle and a fresh, gently sparkling drink results.

Wine

For centuries **Madeira wine** has ensured the island's fame all over the world. It is drunk as an aperitif or digestif rather than with the meal itself (►Baedeker Special, p. 70). Simpler varieties are used in the kitchen, particularly in the preparation of sauces. Madeira wine can be divided into four types: **Malmsey** is the sweetest and probably the best Madeira wine. Characterized by its dark brown tone, its taste has a slight edge. It is an ideal drink when dinner draws to a close. **Bual** is relatively light and not quite as sweet as Malmsey, but is also a fine dessert wine. The aroma of **Verdelho** is a little smoky,

Baedeker TIP

Dentinhos

When ordering a beer or glass of wine in one of the island's simple bars, it is worth asking about »dentinhos« (»little teeth«): the barman will often serve small dishes free of charge, such as tremoços (lupin seeds) or little portions of fish or tripe.

Mixing poncha requires a little elbow grease, but the result is a taste that lives long in the memory

with a trace of honey. It is drunk both as an aperitif and dessert wine. Grapes used in **Sercial** grow on higher ground and are the last to be harvested. The resultant wine is slightly acidic and has a certain lightness, making it the perfect aperitif.

Mineral water (água mineral) is widely available both still and sparkling varieties (com / sem gás). **Beer** (cerveja) is a very popular beverage. Bottled beer is ordered as »cerveja«, whilst draught beer comes in three measures – »imperial« is a small one, »balão« medium, and »caneca« large. As well as imported beers, various Portuguese brews are served on Madeira: Coral, Super Bock and Sagres.

A favourite footnote to an opulent meal is a little glass of **»aguardente«** (literally »fire-water«), a sugarcane spirit that is good for the digestion. Aguardente is also an ingredient in **»poncha«**.

Health

Medical care is provided for throughout Madeira, although the only hospitals are in the capital, Funchal. The larger hotels often have a designated doctor who can be summoned quickly if the need arises. Smaller hotels, guest houses and tourist offices all offer assistance in the event of illness. Otherwise, most places outside Funchal have their own health centres (Centro de Saúde), generally with an emergency unit attached.

Medical care

Pharmacies (farmácias) can be identified by a green and white sign featuring a cross or snake. All medicines manufactured in Portugal are available here, as well as many international compounds. It may be advisable to bring along any more unusual medicines if these are likely to be needed. Opening hours for pharmacies are, as a rule, Mon – Fri 9am – 1pm and 3pm – 6pm, Sat 9am – 1pm. Outside these hours, a sign normally indicates the whereabouts of the nearest pharmacy on stand-by duty. If there is only one in the vicinity, the telephone number of a practising pharmacist on emergency duty is also listed.

Pharmacies

 IN CASE OF ILLNESS

EMERGENCY

► **General emergency service**
Tel. 112 (free of charge)

HOSPITALS IN FUNCHAL

► **Hospital Cruz de Carvalho**
Avenida Luís de Camões
(close to the hotel zone)
Tel. 291 705 600

► **Clínica de Santa Luzia**
with 24 hour clinic
Rua da Torrinha, 5
Tel. 291 200 000

► **Clínica da Sé**
24 hour clinic
Rua dos Murças, 42
Tel. 291 207 676
Some English speaking doctors
and dentists are on call here.

ON PORTO SANTO

► **Centro de Saúde Porto Santo**
Rua Dr. José Diamantino Lima
Tel. 291 980 060

Hiking

Anyone who visits Madeira should take a hike along one of the levadas (►Baedeker Special, p. 160) at least once. Even the most well-travelled hikers delight in the unique, primordial nature of the territory,

Eldorado for hikers

Proper legwork

An old mule track leads from the Eira do Serrado viewing point to Curral das Freiras. The path is not a difficult one, but it can be hard work: from a height of over 400m/1300ft, it winds its way down steeply to the road and continues to the centre (round trip approx. 3 hours).

which can be savoured on the simplest of walks. Levada hiking tours are marvellously varied and are an ideal way of getting to know the island's different regions beyond the usual tourist attractions. Labourers originally used the pathways along the levadas, that is to say, they were not created as hiking trails – in common with most Mediterranean countries, Madeira has no hiking tradition to speak of. Hence the levada trails are rarely marked and are often poor in quality, leading up steep mountain inclines or cut into sheer cliff faces. They may also not be completely safe, for example when the uphill trail alongside the water channel disappears, and the only means of progress is a balancing act on the levada wall! **A head for heights** and **sure-footedness** are essential. The vagaries of the weather can also bring about rapid changes in the state of the pathways. Barriers send out a clear warning: walkers have fallen to their death on these paths.

Weather   Before undertaking a hike in the mountains, be sure to take note of the weather forecast and **be mindful of any warnings**. Sudden changes in the weather can have fatal consequences!

A levada hike can lead to any number of interesting encounters. This cheerful goat is staying put, however, as he belongs to the levadeiro responsible for this stretch

Sturdy footwear with grip soles should suffice for a walk, but it is worth considering useful items such as a rain cape, weatherproof jacket and maybe hiking socks for a more extensive levada hike. Some levada trails pass through tunnels, so a pocket torch might be an asset. Crossing narrow watercourses can quickly lead to wet feet. There should certainly be space for a **hiking guide** and a **map of trails** in the rucksack. A walking guide is recommended under the heading ► Literature. Books and maps can be purchased in the Madeiran tourist information offices, as well as in bookshops and kiosks.

Equipment

The levada trails described in the tours section which follows are easy to negotiate under normal circumstances and are recommended by the tourist information centres. Exact directions can be found in good hiking guides. It is prudent to ask at one of the tourist information offices to check on the current condition of the levada in question, as there may be some closures due to the weather. Further walks and hikes are suggested as appropriate under Sights from A to Z later on. Those who prefer not to leave anything to chance can take part in one of the many levada walks led by guides.

Recommended hikes

Information

USEFUL ADDRESSES

IN UNITED KINGDOM

► **Portuguese National Tourist Office**
11, Belgrave Square
London, SW1X 8PP
Tel. 020 72 01 66 66
tourism.london@portugalglobal.pt
www.visitportugal.com

► **ATOP (Association of Travel Organisers to Portugal)**
Madeira House
High St, Hook Norton
Oxon OX15 5NH
Tel. 016 08 73 82 86
www.destination-portugal.co.uk

IN CANADA

► **Portuguese Tourism Office**
60 Bloor Street West
Suite 1005
Toronto, ON M4W 3B8
Tel. 416 921 73 76
info@visitportugal.com

IN USA

► **Portuguese Trade and Tourism Office in the USA**
590 Fifth Avenue, 3rd Floor
New York, NY 10036
Tel: (646) 723 0200
www.visitportugal.com

ON MADEIRA

► **Direcção Regional do Turismo da Madeira**
Avenida M. Arriaga, 18
9004-519 Funchal
Tel. 00 351 291 211 900
Fax 00 351 291 232 151

www.madeiratourism.com
www.madeiraislands.travel

INTERNET

► **www.madeiratourism.com**
Official tourism website of
Madeira, with an English version.
General overview on what to see
and where to stay on Madeira,
highly informative.

► **www.madeira-web.com**
Everything about a Madeira
holiday, in English: hotels,
weather, walks and pictures from
live webcams at various locations.

► **www.madeira-island.com**
An English-language guide to
Madeira; with hotels, where to
shop, information on museums
and a list of all the festivals held on
the island.

PORTUGUESE CONSULATES AND EMBASSIES

► **Consulate in Australia**
Level 17, 55 Clarence Street
Sydney N.S.W 2000
Tel. 2 926 221 99
Email: mail@cgsyd.dgaccp.pt

► **Consulate in Canada**
438 University Avenue, Suite 1400,
14th Floor
Toronto
Tel. 416 217 09 66

► **Embassy in Ireland**
15 Leeson Park
Dublin 6
Tel. 1 412 70 40
www.embassyportugal.ie

► **Embassy in the United Kingdom**
11 Belgrave Square
London SW1X 8PP
Tel. 020 / 7235 53 31
Fax 020 / 7245 12 87

► **Consulate General in the United Kingdom**
3 Portland Place
London W1B 3HR
Tel. 020 / 7291 37 70
Fax 020 7291 37 99

► **Embassy in the USA**
2125 Kalorama Road
NW Washington, DC 20008
Tel. 202 328 86 10

CONSULATES ON MADEIRA

► **British Honorary Consulate**
Rua da Alfandega, 10, 3C
9000-059 Funchal
Tel. 291 212 860, email: Britcon.-
Funchal@NetMadeira.com
U.S. Consular Agency
Rua da Alfandega, 10-2F
9000-059 Funchal
Tel. 291 123 5626, fax 291 22 9360

Language

Portuguese and
other languages

Portuguese is spoken in Portugal, in Brazil and in the former Portuguese colonies in Africa. On Madeira, English is the most commonly
understood foreign language, but it is well worth making the effort
to learn at least a few words of Portuguese.

Most Portuguese words place the emphasis on the penultimate syllable. A general rule is: if a word ends with m, s or the vowels a, e, o,
the emphasis is placed on the penultimate syllable. If a word ends with
l, r, z or with an ã, i or u, the last syllable is stressed. Accents indicate
variations in emphasis. A tilde (~) indicates the nasalization of vowels.

Portuguese is a Romance language, with early Celtic, Germanic and
Arabic influences still present. Written Portuguese is readily identi-
fiable as a Romance language and may be fairly comprehensible to
anyone with a grasp of Latin or another Romance language. Spoken
Portuguese, on the other hand, is less fathomable: it sounds almost
like a Slavic language. It is characterized by soft pronunciation, by
syllables that run seamlessly into one another, a proliferation of sibi-
lants and a wealth of differently pronounced vowels. Another feature
is the strong emphasis placed on certain syllables, which often leads
to the following unstressed syllable virtually disappearing.

PORTUGUESE PHRASES

At a glance

Yes/no	Sim/Não
Mrs/Mr	Senhora/Senhor
Perhaps	Talvez
Please	Se faz favor
Thank you	Obrigado/Obrigada
You're welcome	De nada/Não tem de quê
Sorry!	Desculpe!/Desculpa!
Okay!	Está bem/De acordo!
When?	Quando?
Where?	Onde?
Excuse me?	Como?
How much?	Quanto?
Where to?	Aonde? Para onde?
What time is it?	Que horas são?
I don't understand.	Não compreendo.
Do you speak English?	Fala inglês?
Please can you help me?	Pode ajudar-me, se faz favor?
I would like …	Queria …
I like it (don't like it).	(Não) Gosto disto.
Do you have …?	Tem …?
What does it cost?	Quanto custa?

Getting acquainted

Good morning /day/evening!	Bom dia!/Boa tarde!/Boa noite!

Hello!	Olá!
How are you?	Como está?/Como vai?
Fine, thank you. And you?	Bem, obrigado/obrigada. E o senhor/a senhora/você/tu?
Goodbye!/See you soon!	Adeus!/Até logo!/Até à próxima!

Finding the way

left/right	ã esquerda/ã direita
straight on	em frente
close/far	perto/longe
Excuse me, where is …?	Se faz favor, onde está …?
How many kilometres is it from here?	Quantos quilómetros são?
I have broken down.	Tenho uma avaria.
Could you tow me to the next garage?	Pode rebocar-me até à oficina mais próxima?
Is there a garage near here?	Há alguma oficina aqui perto?
Excuse me, where is the nearest petrol station?	Se faz favor, onde ésta a bomba de gasolina mais próxima?
I would like … litres …	Se faz favor … litros de …
…Regular petrol/super/diesel.	…gasolina normal/súper/gasóleo.
…Lead-free/ …leaded.	…sem chumbo/com chumbo.
…with …octane.	…com …octanas.
Fill her up, please.	Cheio, se faz favor.
Help!	Socorro!
Watch out! Vorsicht!	Atenção! Cuidado!
Please quickly call …	Chame depressa …
…an ambulance.	…uma ambulância.
…the police/the fire brigade..	…a polícia/os bombeiros.
It was my/your fault.	A culpa foi minha/sua.
Would you give me your name and address, please?	Pode dizer-me o seu nome e o seu endereço, se faz favor?

Eating out

Please could you tell where I can find …	Pode dizer-me, se faz favor, onde há aqui …
…a good restaurant?	…um bom restaurante?
…an inexpensive restaurant?	…um restaurante não muito caro?
…a typical restaurant?	…um restaurante típico?
Is there a bar here/a café?	Há aqui um bar/um café?
Could you please reserve a table for four persons for this evening?	Pode reservar-nos para hoje à noite uma mesa para quatro pessoas, se faz favor?
Could you please give me a …?	Pode-me dar …, se faz favor?
Knife/fork/spoon	faca/garfo/colher
Glass/plate	copo/prato
Salt	sal

Cheers! .... À sua saúde!
Could we pay, please! .... A conta, se faz favor.
Did you enjoy your meal? .... Estava bom?
The meal was excellent. .... A comida estava êcelente.

Sopas, Entradas / Soups, starters

Açorda .... Bread and garlic soup
Caldo verde .... Portuguese kale soup
Sopa de legumes .... Vegetable soup
Sopa de peixe .... Fish soup
Sopa alentejana .... Garlic soup with egg
Amêijoas .... Cockles
Azcitonas .... Olives
Caracóis .... Snails
Espargos frios .... Cold asparagus
Melão com presunto .... Melon with ham
Pão com manteiga .... Bread and butter
Salada de atum .... Tuna salad
Salada à portuguesa .... Mixed salad
Sardinhas em azeite .... Sardines in olive oil

Peixe e mariscos / Fish and seafood

Amêijoas ao natural .... Cockles
Atum .... Tuna
Bacalhau com todos .... Codfish with garnish
Bacalhau à bráz .... Codfish, fried potato,
                                         scrambled egg
Caldeirada .... Fish stew
Camarão grelhado .... Grilled shrimps
Cataplana .... Mussels, fish or meat, paprika,
                                         onion, potato
Dourada .... Sea bream
Ensopado de enguias .... Eel stew
Espadarte .... Swordfish
Filetes de cherne .... Fillet of grouper
Gambas na grelha .... Grilled prawns
Lagosta cozida .... Boiled lobster
Linguado .... Sole
Lulas à sevilhana .... Baked squid
Méilhões de cebolada .... Mussels with onions
Pargo .... Snapper
Peixe espada .... Scabbard fish
Perca .... Perch
Pescada à portuguesa .... Hake, Portuguese style

Salmão .... Salmon
Sardinhas assadas .... Grilled sardines

Carne e aves / Meat and poultry

Bife à portuguesa .... Portuguese beefsteak
Bife de cebolada .... Steak with onion
Bife de peru .... Turkey steak
Cabrito .... Kid
Carne de porco à Alentejana .... Pork with cockles
Carne na grelha/Churrasco .... Charcoal-grilled meat
Coelho .... Rabbit
Costeleta de cordeiro .... Lamb chop
Costeleta de porco .... Pork chop
Escalope de vitela .... Veal cutlet
Espetadas de carne .... Meat skewer
Fígado de vitela .... Calf's liver
Frango assado .... Roast chicken
Frango na púcara .... Chicken casserole
Iscas .... Braised liver
Lebre .... Hare
Leitão assado .... Roast suckling pig
Lombo de carneiro .... Mutton back
Pato .... Duck
Perdiz .... Partridge
Pimentões recheados .... Stuffed peppers
Porco assado .... Roast pork
Rins .... Kidneys
Tripas .... Tripe

Legumes / Vegetables

Batatas .... Potatoes
Beringelas fritas .... Fried aubergine
Bróculos .... Broccoli
Cogumelos .... Mushrooms
Espargos .... Asparagus
Espinafres .... Spinach
Feijão verde .... Green beans
Pepinos .... Gherkins

Sobremesa / Dessert

Arroz doce .... Rice pudding
Gelado misto .... Ice cream

Leite creme	Crème caramel
Pêra Helena	Pear belle Hélène
Pudim flan	Pudding with caramel sauce
Sorvete	Sorbet
Tarte de amêndoa	Almond cake

Lista de bebidas – List of beverages

Aguardente de figos	Fig brandy
Aguardente velho	Old brandy
Bagaço	Bagasse brandy
Ginjinha	Cherry liqueur
Madeira	Madeira wine
Medronho	Strawberry tree brandy
Porto	Port wine
Cerveja/Imperial	Beer/draught beer
Caneca	large draught beer
Vinho branco/Vinho tinto	White wine/red wine
Vinho verde	Light wine with natural acidity
Água mineral	Mineral water
Bica	Espresso
Café (com leite)	Coffee (with milk)
Chá com leite/limão	Tea with milk/lemon
Galão	Milky coffee in a glass
Meia de leite	Coffee with lots of milk
Garoto	Espresso with milk
Laranjada/Sumo de laranja	Orangeade/Orange juice

Accommodation

Could you please ... recommend?	Se faz favor, pode recomendar-me
...a good hotel/a guesthouse	...um bom hotel?/uma pensão?
Do you still have a room free?	Ainda tem quartos livres?
a single room	um quarto individual
a double room	um quarto de casal
a twin bed room	um quarto con duas camas
with bathroom	com casa de banho
... for one night/week.	...para uma noite/semana.

Doctor / Bank / Post office

Can you recommend a good doctor?	Pode indicar-me um bom médico?
It hurts here.	Dói-me aqui.
Is there a bank here?	Onde há aqui um banco?
Postage stamps	selo

How much does a letter/a postcard cost to England? .... Quanto custa um postal/uma carta para a Inglaterra?

May I send a fax to ... ? .... Posso mandar aqui um fax para ...?

Numbers

0	zero
1	um, uma
2	dois, duas
3	três
4	quatro
5	cinco
6	seis
7	sete
8	oito
9	nove
10	dez
11	onze
12	doze
13	treze
14	catorze
15	quinze
16	dezasseis
17	dezassete
18	dezoito
19	dezanove
20	vinte
30	trinta
40	quarenta
50	cinquenta
60	sessenta
70	setenta
80	oitenta
90	noventa
100	cem
101	cento e um
200	duzentos
1000	mil
2000	dois mil
1/2	um meio
1/3	um terço
1/4	um quarto

Days of the week

Segunda-feira .... Monday

Terça-feira	Tuesday
Quarta-feira	Wednesday
Quinta-feira	Thursday
Sexta-feira	Friday
Sábado	Saturday
Domingo	Sunday
Feriado	Holiday

Literature

Christopher Columbus: Logbook. Penguin Classics, 1992
For anyone wishing to delve deeper into the voyages of discovery of
Christopher Columbus.

John and Pat Underwood: Madeira: Car Tours and Walks, Sunflower
Books 2010.
10th edition of a classic guide to walking on the island.

Background
information

Gerald Luckhurst: The Gardens of Madeira, Frances Lincoln 2010
30 gardens on the island, described by an expert.

Tony Clarke: Field Guide to the Birds of the Atlantic Islands, A&C
Black, 2006. Up-to-date work describing all species found on the Ma
caronesian islands, i.e. the Canaries, Madeira, Azores and Cape Verde.

Marcus Binney: The Blandys of Madeira: 1811-2011, Frances Lincoln
2011. 200 years of a company and family that has shaped the history
of the island and its famous wine.

Media

Most hotels and apartments receive **foreign-language channels**.
Portuguese television comprises two state channels, RTP 1 and 2
(culture), as well as various private stations such as SIC and TVI.
Foreign films are usually broadcast in their original language with
subtitles.

Radio and
television
Television

English daily newspapers and weekly magazines can be purchased at
virtually every newsstand or kiosk in Funchal, as well as in many hotels. Daily papers tend to arrive on the island a day after publication,

Newspapers and
magazines

however. Visitors to Madeira will find **Soft Madeira News Magazine and _Madeira Life_**, published in English, of interest. The latter incorporates listings for forthcoming events over the next couple of months, a basic bus timetable and useful telephone numbers (taxi, hospital, police station). Madeira's daily newspapers are the _Jornal da Madeira_ and _Diário de Notícias_ with a weather chart, cruise ship timetables and useful telephone numbers.

Money

Euro Since 2002, the euro has been legal tender. The national faces of the Portuguese euro coins depict three seals of the founder of the Portuguese kingdom, King Afonso Henriques from the 12th century.

Banks Banks are open Mon – Fri 8.30am – 5pm, although many close for lunch between 12.30pm and 2pm.

Cash machines, credit cards The easiest way to pick up cash is from a cash machine (ATM) (»Multibanco«, maximum 200€), with instructions in several languages. EC cards (standard charge approx. 4€), bank cards and credit cards (using the latter can be very expensive!) are all accepted in conjunction with a PIN number. Banks, the larger hotels, high-class restaurants, car rental companies and some of the bigger specialist stores accept most internationally recognized credit cards. Visa and Eurocard are widespread, American Express and Diners Club less so.

▶ CONTACT DETAILS FOR CREDIT CARDS

In the event of lost bank or credit cards you can contact the following numbers in UK and USA (phone numbers when dialling from Madeira):

▶ **Eurocard/MasterCard**
Tel. 001 / 636 7227 111

▶ **Visa**
Tel. 001 / 410 581 336

▶ **American Express UK**
Tel. 0044 / 1273 696 933

▶ **American Express USA**
Tel. 001 / 800 528 4800

▶ **Diners Club UK**
Tel. 0044 / 1252 513 500

▶ **Diners Club USA**
Tel. 001 / 303 799 9000
Have the bank sort code, account number and card number as well as the expiry date ready.

The following numbers of UK banks (dialling from Madeira) can be used to report and cancel lost or stolen bank and credit cards issued by those banks:

▶ **HSBC**
Tel. 0044 / 1442 422 929

► **Barclaycard**
Tel. 0044 / 1604 230 230

► **NatWest**
Tel. 0044 / 142 370 0545

► **Lloyds TSB**
Tel. 0044 / 1702 278 270

 Exchange rates

■ Euro 1 = GBP 0.85
GBP 1 = Euro 1.18
Euro 1 = US-$ 1.33
US-$ 1 = Euro 0.75

Post and Communications

Post offices can be identified by the sign »correio« (Portuguese for post office). Opening hours are usually Mon – Fri 9am – 12.30pm and 2.30pm – 6pm. The post office in the Avenida Zarco in the centre of Funchal is open all day Mon – Fri 9am – 8pm and 9am – 6pm on Saturdays and Sundays.   **Post offices**

For letters (cartas) and postcards (postais) within Europe, postage costs 61 cents. (selos) can be purchased in post offices or in shops bearing the sign »CTT Selos«. Allow around a week for letters and postcards to reach their destination. The more expensive »correio azul« is somewhat faster.   **Postage**

Almost all public telephones on Madeira have been converted from coin-operated models to telephone cards (»Telecom Card« or »cartão para telefonar«), which can be purchased in post offices or kiosks.   **Public telephones**

 DIALLING CODES

**FROM MADEIRA /
PORTO SANTO**

► **to Canada/USA**
Tel. 001

► **to United Kingdom**
Tel. 0044

► **to Ireland**
Tel. 00353
The zero of the local code should be omitted.

**TO MADEIRA /
PORTO SANTO**

► **From outside Portuguese territory**
Tel. 00351
followed by the nine digit number, which begins with 291 on Madeira and Porto Santo.

Mobile phones Network coverage is good in urban areas, but less reliable in the more remote regions. No international dialling code is required, just add 291 before the number you wish to call. To call a mobile phone, just dial the nine-digit number. The major Portuguese network operators are TMN (Telemovel), Optimus and Vodafone. Advice on the cheapest operator can be obtained from your own provider.

Prices and Discounts

Tipping In cafés and bars it is customary to leave a few coins on the table or on the counter, whilst in restaurants a tip of between 5% and 10% is appropriate. At the end of a taxi ride, round up the amount accordingly. Chambermaids, porters or tourist guides on sightseeing trips will appreciate a tip of two or three euros.

 WHAT DOES IT COST?

Three-course meal
from € 15

Simple meal
from € 7

Espresso
from € 1

Bus trip
from € 1.50

Basic double room
from € 50

Glass of beer/ 285 ml
from € 2

Shopping

Shopping in Funchal The centre of Funchal boasts a wealth of shops – everything from small bric-a-brac stores to fashion emporia purveying internationally renowned labels. The Santa Quitéria shopping centre outside Funchal offers a wide variety under one roof. In the west of Funchal, the hotel zone is a good place for a shopping trip. There are also many observation points on the island complemented by large souvenir shops, all with similar wares on display.

A hugely popular holiday gift is, of course, Madeira wine (► Baedeker Special, p. 70).

Among Madeira's classic souvenirs are the marvellous examples of white work: intricately embroidered items of clothing and table linen. Only those carrying a **certificate of authenticity** issued by the Institute for Handicrafts (IBTAM) are the genuine article. Those interested in tapestry will enjoy the selection of »old masters« in needlepoint.

More practical holiday gifts include goatskin boots (botas), woollen bobble hats with earflaps and lambswool jackets. Various liqueurs or a »brinquinho«, a kind of Turkish crescent (► Arts and Culture, p. 46) available in almost all souvenir shops, are also excellent buys.

Practical and miscellaneous

Another well-liked, if bulky souvenir is basketwork from Camacha. When buying larger products – such as a full complement of chairs or a suite – shipment can be arranged by the sales staff in Café Relógio (► Sights from A to Z: Camacha), who will take care of all the formalities.

Basketwork

Flowers, such as bird of paradise flowers, orchids or proteas, are also popular souvenirs and can be bought in Funchal flower shops or, for a wider selection, in the Mercado dos Lavradores or – the last chance – from a small shop in the departure hall at the airport. Orchids for cultivation are on sale in the Orchid Garden (► Sights from A to Z, around Funchal, p. 150). Bags of seeds are also on offer in various places.

Madeiran **postage stamps** are renowned for often featuring large and colourful flora and fauna motifs, making them sought-after souvenirs, not only for philatelists. A good place to purchase them is the philately department of the main post office in Funchal.

! **Baedeker TIP**

Chestnut liqueur and fennel sweets
The tasty chestnuts that grow on the trees around Curral das Freiras form the basis of fine local specialities: sample the celebrated chestnut liqueur at least once. If you have a sweet tooth candidates, choose between fennel and eucalyptus sweets – or try both.

The »brinquinho« is a unique form of Turkish crescent

Sport & Fun

The tourist office in Funchal has a brochure with information on various sporting activities.

Angling, deep-sea fishing
Deep-sea fishing trips – for a full or half day – are offered by various agencies at Funchal harbour. Hotels will provide assistance in looking for and confirming bookings. With a little luck, dolphins or even whales will come into view.

Cycling
Cycling is gaining in popularity on Madeira. Numerous hotels rent out bicycles, and further assistance is available from tourist information office. Madeira's motorists are not necessarily used to the presence of cyclists, but with new roads and tunnels attracting through-traffic, many a coastal road can be considered for a bike ride, the stretch between Ponta do Sol and Madalena do Mar being a prime example. Whereas the topography of the island is predominantly suited to proficient or seasoned cyclists, the more even terrain of Porto Santo is easier to negotiate: almost half of the 10km/6mi-long route commencing at the harbour and following the sandy beach to Calheta consists of a designated cycle track (►Baedeker Tip p. 179).

The Santo da Serra golf course has 18 holes and wonderful views of Madeira's eastern peninsula

Cycling, surfing or swimming – sports enthusiasts will find plenty to keep them occupied

Madeira is home to two outstandingly landscaped golf courses. The slightly older of the two, in Santo da Serra (►Sights from A – Z, Santo da Serra) is famous for its location at a height of 670m/2100ft and stunning views (p. 90). The 27-hole complex was designed by Robert Trent Jones. A hilly 18-hole course lies alongside the Quinta do Palheiro above Funchal. In 2004 Porto Santo also got a golf course of its own: with the Spanish champion Severiano Ballesteros acting as a design consultant, an 18-hole course and pitch and putt (under floodlights) were created between Capela de São Pedro and the north coast. A second 18-hole course close by is in the planning stages.

Golf

For experienced riders, Madeira is a veritable paradise. Narrow, steep and winding roads, damp tunnels and intermittent banks of mist, the unorthodox Portuguese style of driving and the odd cow on the asphalt provide real challenges to the most capable of bikers.

Motorbikes

Mountain bike tours on Madeira are not for novices. Before taking on any tours, guided or otherwise, a good 1000km/600mi of pedal work should be a minimum requirement. With that, fun and adventure are guaranteed.

Mountain biking

Sailors can aim for the Funchal Marina with some 130 mooring berths, the new marinas of Calheta, Lugar do Baixo, east of Ponta do Sol, and Porto Moniz, as well as the marina of Porto Santo. A yachtmaster certificate is required to rent a sailing boat. Information can be obtained from tourist offices.

Sailing

Windsurfing
Madeira's rocky coastline does not provide ideal conditions for windsurfers. The waves on the north coast are liable to be too violent and the winds on the south coast too weak. The beach at Porto Santo is far better territory. Skilled boarders, however, like to meet at Jardim do Mar and Paúl do Mar.

Diving
The Atlantic Ocean around Madeira and Porto Santo offers a whole world of experience for divers. Some companies have specialized in diving expeditions and equipment rental.

Tennis
All of the bigger hotels have their own tennis courts and equipment for hire; some hotels offer tennis coaching. There are also public tennis courts in Funchal and elsewhere.

Football
Madeirans love their football. The Estádio dos Barreiros lies to the north of the hotel zone on the Rua do Dr. Pita. Both Madeiran clubs, Marítimo Funchal and Nacional Funchal, play in Portugal's Superliga. Details of upcoming fixtures can be obtained from the tourist information offices or hotel receptions.

Hiking
►p. 75, 110

Time

Madeira and the Portuguese mainland
Madeira, like the Portuguese mainland, observes Western European Time (WET = Greenwich Mean Time). Summer time also applies from the end of March until the end of October, so visitors from Britain need not reset their watches.

Transport

Driving

Traffic regulations
On Madeira – as in the rest of Portugal – vehicles drive on the right. Within urban areas, the speed limit is 50kmh/31mph; elsewhere on trunk roads the maximum is 90kmh/56 mph, rising to 100kmh/62mph on fast roads. The wearing of seat belts is compulsory. Motorcyclists must wear a helmet. Telephoning is only permitted with a hands-free system. Driving with a blood alcohol level of 0.5 millilitres or more is an offence. A hi-visibility vest and warning triangle must be kept in the vehicle.

Road conditions
Those unfamiliar with the roads should adhere to a **careful driving style**. Many of the old roads on Madeira are narrow and winding,

and a speeding vehicle may pop up in the wrong lane at any moment. In recent times, the situation has been eased by the ongoing construction of faster roads and numerous tunnels. Funchal traffic now flows faster thanks to the Via à Cota 40 and the even newer Via à Cota 200, which bypasses the centre with a series of tunnels.

With a less than perfect system of road signs, it is always a good idea to carry a map, particularly in view of the extensive construction work of recent years. Older roads are often narrow, and when they lead to tourist attractions and expect to meet many cars or buses coming in the opposite direction. In especially narrow spots, **passing places** ease the situation. Whichever vehicle is closer to a passing point is expected to reverse. On an incline, the vehicle driving up the hill is expected to give way. Minor **landslips** occur on many of the steeper roads. Small **waterfalls** flow directly onto the roads in some places and water sometimes drips from above in older tunnels. If a road becomes impassable and is temporarily closed, there is no alternative but to turn back. Continuing at one's own risk may put lives in danger.

Road map

There are plenty of petrol stations in Funchal, but not so many further away. Most petrol stations are open until 10pm, some until midnight. Lead-free petrol is available as »gasolina sem chumbo 95« and »gasolina sem chumbo 98«.

Fuel

A variety of **local and international car rental companies** are represented in Funchal, especially in the hotel zone to the west of the centre, and local suppliers can be found in almost all the larger spots on the island. Hire car rates are fairly reasonable. A compact vehicle costs around 25–35€ plus tax per day. A valid driving licence is required and the minimum age for drivers is 21. Rental companies often insist on 12 months driving experience. Third-party insurance is statutory, comprehensive cover is recommended. If any problems arise with the vehicle, check with the rental company. In the event of an accident, contact the police.

Car hire

Madeiran taxis are yellow. Taxi rides are not too expensive, but beware of some rather imaginative prices, particularly in Funchal. A list of set journey prices on the island is available, with taxi ranks located on the square in front of the town hall, for example, and on the Avenida Arriaga by the Jardim Municipal. Longer excursions with a taxi are also a possibility. Take a ride to the beginning of a levada hike, for instance, and arrange a collection at the destination.

Taxi

⏵ RENTAL CARS

LOCAL AGENTS

▶ **Rodavante**
Aeroporto da Madeira
Tel. 291 524 718
Fax 291 524 762

Aeroporto do Porto Santo
Tel. 291 982 925

Estr. Monumental, 306
Hotel Florasol, Funchal
Tel. 291 764 361
www.rodavante.com

▶ **Moinho**
Hotel Vila Baleira
Loja 1, Porto Santo
Tel. 291 982 141
Fax 291 982 717

Aeroporto de Porto Santo
Tel. 291 983 260
moinho@moinho-rentacar.com
www.moinhorentacar.com

▶ **Magoscar**
Caniço: Apartado 46

Tel. 291 934 818
www.magoscar.com

INTERNATIONAL

▶ **Avis**
Tel. (UK) 08700 100 287
www.avis.com
Funchal Flughafen
Tel. 291 524 382
Largo António Nobre, 164
Tel. 291 764 546
Estrada Monumental 284
Tel. 291 776 360

▶ **Europcar**
Tel. (UK) 08713 849 847
www.europcar.co.uk
Funchal City
Tel. 291 765 116

▶ **Hertz**
Tel. (UK 24hrs) 0843 309 3009
www.hertz.co.uk
Funchal: Airport
Tel. 291 523 040

Public Transport

In Funchal and across the country

Madeira's public transport network is relatively well developed, if somewhat complex. Funchal's municipal bus service is generally efficient.

Buses (autocarros) go to all places on the island, sometimes admittedly at snail's pace. Careful planning is necessary, as in some cases services to the more remote spots run only once per day. Six private bus companies are based in Funchal. They have various different points of departure, although most start from the Avenida do Mar. Funchal has **no central bus station**. Take care to note the destination as marked on the bus, as the municipal and cross-country services sometimes use the same numbers! Almost all bus routes are out of service on 25 December and, to a slightly lesser extent, on 31 December. Departure times, timetables and further details can be ob-

⏵ SELECTED BUS ROUTES

IN FUNCHAL

▶ **Routes 1, 2 and 6**
Intra-urban routes to the hotel zone

CROSS-COUNTRY

▶ **Route 6**
Funchal – Boaventura
(via São Vicente)

▶ **Route 7**
Funchal – Ribeira Brava

▶ **Route 8**
Funchal – Madalena do Mar

▶ **Route 20, 21**
Funchal – Monte

▶ **Routes 29, 30, 31**
Funchal – Jardim Botânico

▶ **Routes 29, 77**
Funchal – Camacha

▶ **Route 56**
Funchal – Santana (express service via airport and Machico)

▶ **Route 77**
Funchal – Santo da Serra

▶ **Route 80**
Funchal – Porto Moniz (via Ribeira Brava, Ponta do Sol Prazeres), return via Seixal, São Vicente, Ribeira Brava)

▶ **Route 81**
Funchal – Curral das Freiras

▶ **Route 103**
Funchal – Arco de São Jorge
(via airport)

Keep well to the right and no overtaking ...

▶ **Route 113**
Funchal – Santa Cruz
(via airport)

▶ **Route 115**
Funchal – Jardim do Mar

▶ **Route 139**
Funchal – Paúl da Serra – Porto
Moniz – São Vicente – Serra
d'Água – Funchal

▶ **Route 142**
Funchal – Ponta do Pargo (via
Ribeira Brava, Ponta do Sol,
Cadhlheta)

▶ **Route 154**
Funchal – Cabo Girão

▶ **Route 155**
Funchal – Caniço de Baixo

tained from the tourist information offices (▶Information). The plan
for Funchal indicates routes to the most important tourist spots. For
journeys within Funchal, a 7-day ticket is worth considering for
those not living immediately in the centre.
On **Porto Santo**, four bus routes depart daily from Vila Baleira to various places on the island.

Bus stops   Bus stops are usually, but not always, marked by a »paragem« sign –
in isolated locations, some detective work may be required. Timetables and departure times are displayed at bus stops – depending on
the bus company, departure times from the starting point of the
route may also be listed. It is advisable to signal to the bus to stop,
otherwise it may simply drive past.

Travellers with Disabilities

On account of its topography, Madeira is rather **difficult terrain** for
travellers with disabilities. The steep paths and roads and a proliferation of cobblestones make the going tough, not just for the wheel-
chair-bound. To date, few hotels have full accessibility facilities. The
situation is improving, albeit relatively slowly.

▶ **INFORMATION FOR THE DISABLED**

UNITED KINGDOM

▶ **Tourism for All**
c/o Vitalise, Shap Road Industrial
Estate, Shap Road, Kendal
Cumbria LA9 6NZ
Tel. 08 45 124 99 71
www.tourismforall.org.uk

USA

▶ **SATH (Society for Accessible
Travel and Hospitality)**
347 5th Ave., no. 605
New York, NY 10016:
Tel. (212) 4 47 72 84
www.sath.org

Levada hikes are nigh on impossible for those with limited mobility, as the trails are usually far too narrow. On the plus side, a **hiking trail through the laurisilva forest** from Pico das Pedras to Queimadas, almost 2 km/over a mile long, has been made suitable for wheelchairs.

When to Go

Thanks to its favourable climate, the island is worth a visit at any time of year. Even in winter, temperatures only drop to European levels in the upper regions of the island, whilst in Funchal, for example, the thermometer rarely dips below 18°C/64°F (▶ Natural Environment, p. 17).

An island for any time of year

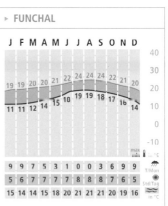

▶ FUNCHAL

With Madeira being such a popular **summer** destination not only for sunseeking Europeans, but also for the Portuguese themselves, the island is undeniably busy during the Portuguese summer holidays, but never overcrowded. Nevertheless, if at all possible avoid July and August, especially on the neighbouring island of Porto Santo with its long stretches of sandy beach. The peak season on Madeira also encompasses the week from **Christmas** to **New Year**. The island is busier in this period and prices somewhat higher.

From April to June and again from September until the beginning of November, the number of holidaymakers decreases considerably. Visiting the island at this time has the added bonus of seeing Madeira in full bloom, and the sun is less intense.

Low season

Although Madeira is **in bloom all year round**, it can still be interesting to find out what is blossoming on the island at any given time. When the jacaranda trees reveal their violet blossoms in April/May, for example, Funchal looks particularly attractive. Roadsides and some of the levadas are adorned with blossoming hydrangeas and agapanthus in August/September. Camellia enthusiasts should come in winter.

? DID YOU KNOW …?

■ The Ilhas Desertas are a good means of gauging the weather: if they appear close and a hazy line can be seen on the horizon, then rain is probably on the way. Should they rise indistinctly from the mist, then the weather is likely to remain fine.

Tours

ON THESE TOURS, YOU WILL
BECOME ACQUAINTED WITH
THE ISLAND'S SPLENDID DIVERSITY –
DISCOVER YOUR OWN FAVOURITE
SPOT, AS WINSTON CHURCHILL
DID LONG AGO!

TOURS THROUGH MADEIRA

These four tours are not for those in a hurry. Take time to marvel at the splendid natural landscape, to enjoy the island's daily life and hidden treasures.

■■■■ **TOUR 1** **Through the mountains to the eastern peninsula**
Lovers of basketry and whales will find much to their taste on this tour. After a bite to eat in Machico, the trail continues to the magnificent easternmost point of the island, before returning at a leisurely pace. ► **page 102**

■■■■ **TOUR 2** **The heart of the island – south coast, north coast and the mountains**
Marvellous views in all directions can be enjoyed on this tour from Cabo Girão on the south coast, along the Encumeada Pass through the mountains to »As Cabanas« on the north coast, with delightful coastal villages, lava caves and a famous pilgrimage church. ► **page 104**

■■■■ **TOUR 3** **Wild north coast and rough mountain terrain**
A spectacular coastal route, lava swimming pools fashioned by nature, highlands reminiscent of Scotland and a magnificent mountain pass are the highlights of this tour. ► **page 107**

■■■■ **TOUR 4** **To the end of the island and back across the mountains**
Pretty villages and fishing settlements are dotted along the south coast, where the end of the Old World is marked by a lighthouse with a bright red top. The return leg crosses green highlands and a tremendous mountain pass. ► **page 108**

Kids also enjoy hiking near Rabaçal

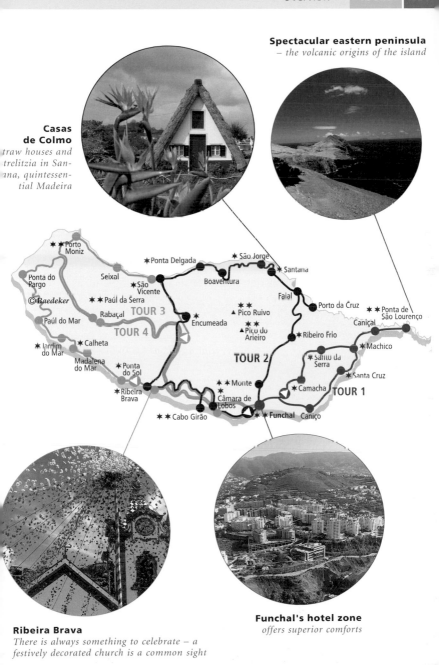

Spectacular eastern peninsula
– the volcanic origins of the island

Casas de Colmo
traw houses and trelitzia in Sanana, quintessential Madeira

Ribeira Brava
There is always something to celebrate – a festively decorated church is a common sight

Funchal's hotel zone
offers superior comforts

Holiday on Madeira

North or south coast

North or south coast, that is the question on Madeira. Most holiday-makers are sure to seek accommodation in or around Funchal. The range of hotels here is matched by a varied cultural life. Those who relish rest and relaxation, waves crashing along a rocky coastline or are particularly looking forward to hiking across the »green pearl in the ocean« should take a closer look at what the north coast has to offer.

Rocky coast and high mountains

Madeira does not match the common perception of an island as an endless succession of sandy beaches, but the neighbouring island fits the bill. Porto Santo has around 9km/5.5mi of sands, offering ample beach space for everybody, even at the height of summer when the Portuguese take their holidays. Madeira, on the other hand, is home to a spectacular rocky coastline with, at best, pebble beaches and natural bathing pools for keen swimmers, not to mention cosy fishing villages, magnificent highlands, lush nature in full bloom and at its heart the lively capital Funchal with its diverse cultural offerings.

The tours in question ...

All of the tours suggested here begin and end in Funchal, but the routes can be joined at different points along the way and, in most cases, combined with each other. It is worth noting that the roads on these itineraries are often narrow and winding, hence the journeys may take some time. Madeira's roads are in good condition, yet often steep, narrow and serpentine. Minor roads are sometimes paved rather than asphalted. New tunnels and expressways have reduced transit times to most destinations on the island. The older roads, where feasible, are more suited to the purpose of sightseeing.

Tour 1 Through the mountains to the eastern peninsula

Start and finish: Funchal **Length:** 1 day
Length: 80km/50mi

This tour leads through the mountainous eastern region of Madeira to the impressive landscape of the peninsula in the east and along the coast back to Funchal.

From ❶ ✷ ✷ **Funchal**, head northeast on the ER 102. First port of call is ❷ ✷ **Camacha**, the basketry centre of Madeira. The 102 leads northwards through mountain forests. Turn onto the smaller 207 and continue through secluded forests to ❸ ✷ **Santo da Serra**. A

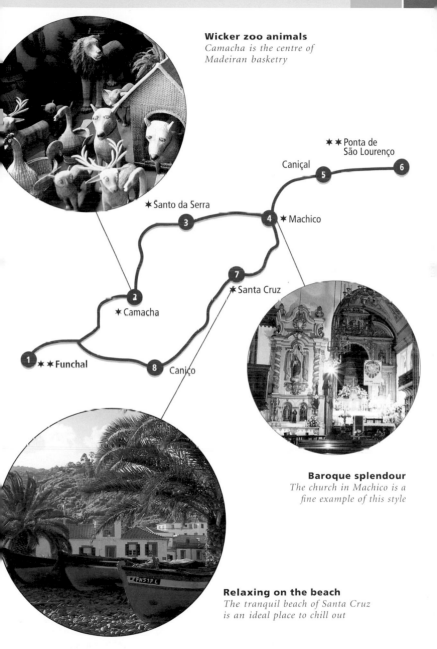

Wicker zoo animals
*Camacha is the centre of
Madeiran basketry*

**✳✳ Ponta de
São Lourenço**

Caniçal

5

6

✳ Santo da Serra

3

4 ✳ Machico

7

✳ Santa Cruz

2

✳ Camacha

1 ✳✳ Funchal

8 Caniço

Baroque splendour
*The church in Machico is a
fine example of this style*

Relaxing on the beach
*The tranquil beach of Santa Cruz
is an ideal place to chill out*

road here connects to the ER 108, which twists and turns its way down from the mountains before shortly reaching picturesque ❹✶ **Machico** on the coast. This little town was once the seat of government for eastern Madeira. In this period the parish church of Nossa Senhora da Conceição was established, featuring remarkable wood carving from the late 15th century. The bars in the old centre of Machico between the church and the fort are ideal for a short break. Suitably re- freshed, continue to the eastern corner of Madeira: pass through the tunnel to ❺ **Caniçal** with its small whale museum before fol- lowing the road to its conclusion on the eastern peninsula, where ❻✶✶ **Ponta de São Lourenço** reaches out to the sea across the rocks.

The return leg again passes through Caniçal and Machico before joining the ER 101 towards Funchal. It is worth stopping off in ❼✶ **Santa Cruz** to admire the notable 16th-century church and attractive pebble beach. The monumental statue of Christ can be reached via ❽ **Caniço**, which lies beyond the airport at Santa Catarina. Caniço is also home to a pretty Baroque church. A few miles further down, on the coast, lies Caniço de Baixo, one of the island's main tourist centres. Funchal is situated just a few miles to the west.

DON'T MISS

- The basket weaving centre in Camacha
- Strolling through Machico
- A walk to the eastern point of Madeira
- Relaxing on the beach at Santa Cruz

Tour 2 The heart of the island – south coast, north coast and the mountains

Start and finish: Funchal
Distance: 140km/85mi

Length: 1 day is possible if sightseeing stops are not too long. 2 days with an overnight stay (in Boaventura, for example) would be a more leisurely option.

This brisk one-day itinerary has everything: a lovely drive along the impressive south coast, two lively little coastal towns, magnificent panoramic views from the heights of a pass, lava caves, volcanoes, snug straw huts, the dramatic rock formations of the north coast and a winding route back to the capital.

Head west from ❶✶✶ **Funchal** on the coastal road ER 229 with its splendid views before arriving in ❷✶ **Câmara de Lobos** just a few miles further on. This small picturesque fishing harbour is situated below the eastern face of the Cabo Girão cliff. Beyond Câmara de Lobos the road winds its way up and away from the coast to Estreito

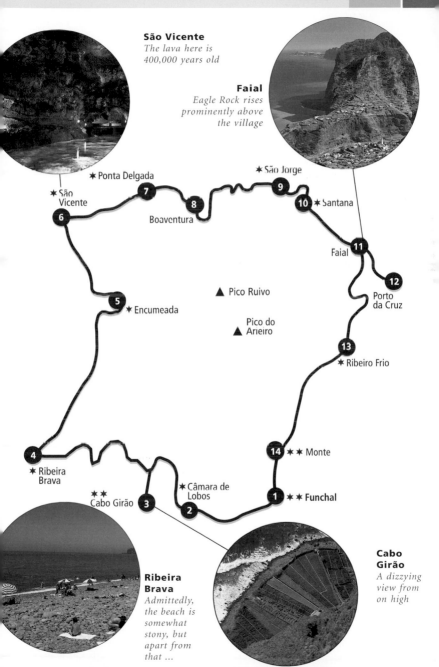

São Vicente
The lava here is 400,000 years old

Faial
Eagle Rock rises prominently above the village

★ São Jorge

★ Ponta Delgada

9

7

★ São Vicente

8

10 ★ Santana

6

Boaventura

11

Faial

12

▲ Pico Ruivo

Porto da Cruz

5 ★ Encumeada

Pico do
▲ Arieiro

13

★ Ribeiro Frio

4

★ Ribeira Brava

14 ★★ Monte

★★
Cabo Girão

3

★ Câmara de Lobos

1 ★★ **Funchal**

2

Ribeira Brava
Admittedly, the beach is somewhat stony, but apart from that ...

Cabo Girão
A dizzying view from on high

de Câmara de Lobos, a village renowned for its wine. After approximately 4km/2.5mi, a road branches off to the left, leading to a viewing point across the **❸✶✶ Cabo Girão**, a sea cliff rising vertically from the water to a height of 589m/1932ft and forming part of one of the steepest coastlines in Europe. The coast road finally reaches **❹✶ Ribeira Brava**, a lively little town picturesquely located on the river estuary of the same name (please note: the new express route through the tunnel bypasses the town, so keep an eye out for the correct turn-off). The parish church of São Bento, dating back to the 16th century, merits a visit. The pyramidal roof of its tower is tiled blue and white. On leaving Ribeira Brava, follow the ER 104 north towards São Vicente as it makes its way inland along the Ribeira Brava river and gradually climbs into a superb mountain landscape. At Serra de Água, there is a decision to be made: the fast road or the scenic route? The ER 228 is by far the more attractive and rewarding alternative, passing through a breathtaking mountainous region, over the **❺✶ Encumeada Pass** and down again to **❻✶ São Vicente**; the faster route continues along the ER 104 through a tunnel approximately 3km/2mi long. Once a simple fishing village, the centre of São Vicente has been spruced up into a popular tourist destination, with lava caves and a Volcanism Centre on the outskirts.

DON'T MISS

- The view from Cabo Girão;
- Panoramic view at Encumeada Pass
- Lava caves at São Vicente
- Casas de Colmo in Santana
- Eagle Rock at Faial
- Pilgrimage church in Monte

Now take the ER 101 leading eastwards to **❼✶ Ponta Delgada**. Ponta Delgada is a charming village nestled on a headland between sugar cane fields, with a pilgrimage church in a lovely spot overlooking the sea and a seawater swimming pool. Beyond the village, the road leaves the coast on a wide curve inland. Just over a mile, it reaches **❽ Boaventura**, both peaceful and pretty; the landscape here is dominated by fruit plantations and willows, the latter mainly for the basketry trade in Camacha. On the ER 101 past Arco de São Jorge lies the As Cabanas viewpoint, with its celebrated panorama of the north coast. In **❾✶ São Jorge** it is worth visiting the exceptionally grand Baroque church before continuing just a few miles to **❿✶ Santana**, famous for its thatched houses with roofs that reach right down to the ground. The coastal road beyond Santana offers unbroken views of considerable beauty before **⓫ Faial** is reached soon afterwards. Some 150m/490ft above sea level, it is surrounded by wine terraces, sugarcane and vegetable fields. The view from the church terrace is splendid. Next, it is worth venturing southeast to **⓬ Porto da Cruz** with its seawater swimming pool, passing the unusual form of the 594m/1948ft Penha de Águia (Eagle Rock). Back in Faial, the ER 103 goes via the trout farms in the countryside around **⓭✶ Ribeiro Frio** and **⓮✶✶ Monte** with its famous pilgrimage church, as it makes its way back to Funchal.

Tour 3 Wild north coast and rough mountain terrain

Start and finish: Funchal
Distance: 120km/75mi

Length: 1 day

This tour is dedicated to the scenic beauty of the north coast and the plateau in the west of the island. Hence the fastest route from Funchal to the north coast is recommended. The alternative route to the north coast may be more attractive, but it also takes far longer and is realistic only for early risers.

Misty images
Lava rocks at Porto Moniz

Mountain images
The coast at Seixal

4 ★★ Porto Moniz

Seixal
3

★São Vicente
2

5

Rabaçal

Landscape images
Hiking at Rabaçal

★★Funchal
1

The quickest way to reach the north coast leads west from ❶✶✶ **Funchal** through the many tunnels of the Via Cota 200 and the R 101, which joins the ER 104 at Ribeira Brava. In no time at all, this arrives – by way of another tunnel – in ❷✶ **São Vicente**.

The 101 then follows the coast westwards through ❸**Seixal** and Ribeira da Janela to ❹✶✶ **Porto Moniz**. The scenery along this coastal road is truly magnificent. Again, there is a fast route and a scenic one.

If at all possible, do not pass up the opportunity of bathing in the lava rock pools of Porto Moniz. The 101 then leaves Porto Moniz and winds southwest up the mountainside. About 2km/just over a mile beyond Santa Madalena, turn left onto the 110, which leads up quickly to the Paúl da Serra plateau. At ❺**Rabaçal** there is a challenging hike to the 25 Fontes, or an easier walk to the Risco waterfall. At the Encumeada Pass, with wonderful views of the north and south coast, the 110 meets the 228, which leads through fragrant eucalyptus woods and down to Serra de Água. To return to Funchal, take the 104 and the 101.

✓ DON'T MISS

- ▪ Volcanism Centre in São Vicente
- ▪ Lava swimming pools in Porto Moniz
- ▪ Hiking near Rabaçal

Tour 4 To the end of the island and back across the mountains

Start and finish: Funchal **Length:** 1 day – with an early start
Distance: 120km/75mi

This tour passes through various small villages on the south coast en route to Madeira's westernmost point, before heading inland across the plateau. Instead of going all the way west, it is possible to turn off early to the Paúl da Serra plateau via the 209, 210 or 211.

From ❶✶✶ **Funchal** take the 101 coastal road west to ❷✶ **Câmara de Lobos**, where Churchill liked to stay, then from ❸✶ **Ribeira Brava** to ❹✶ **Ponta do Sol**, with its beautiful riverside and lovely church. West of Ponta do Sol lies charming ❺**Madalena do Mar**, where time seems to have stood still.

Follow the 101 coast road to ❻✶ **Calheta**, once a centre of sugarcane cultivation that now attracts visitors with its artificial sandy beach. The coastal road twists and turns upwards to Estreito da Calheta before a side road branches off to ❼✶ **Jardim do Mar**, where local surfers congregate on the pebble beaches before taking on the mighty

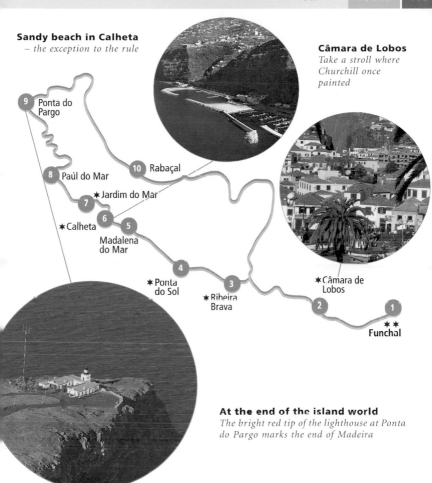

Sandy beach in Calheta
– the exception to the rule

Câmara de Lobos
*Take a stroll where
Churchill once
painted*

9 Ponta do Pargo

10 Rabaçal

8 Paúl do Mar

★ Jardim do Mar

7

6

★ Calheta

5

Madalena
do Mar

4

★ Ponta
do Sol

3

★ Ribeira
Brava

★ Câmara de
Lobos

2

1

★★
Funchal

At the end of the island world
*The bright red tip of the lighthouse at Ponta
do Pargo marks the end of Madeira*

waves. A tunnel leads to ❽**Paúl do Mar**; the 223 then leaves the coast, winding its way up to the 101. It is easy to lose count of the bends by the time ❾**Ponta do Pargo** appears, its lighthouse marking the westernmost point of Madeira. Further on towards Porto Moniz, the 110 branches off at a considerable height above the town. This road traverses the Paúl da Serra plateau, past ❿**Rabaçal,** and meets the 229 at the Encumeada Pass before descending the valley to Serra de Água. The 104 and 101 complete the circuit to Funchal.

✔ **DON'T MISS**

■ Câmara de Lobos harbour
■ Sandy beach in Calheta
■ Ponta do Pargo lighthouse

Hiking on Madeira

From Funchal to the Socorridos Valley

This is a highly popular hiking trail, as it begins in Funchal above the hotel zone and can be concluded with a bus ride from Pinheiro das Voltas back to town. However, the trail which follows the Levada dos Piornais and the Levada do Curral takes some time before it leaves the town and ventures into more attractive territory. A head for heights is undoubtedly an asset, even if the path is secure. Allow four to five hours in total.

Along the Levada dos Tornos

This trail leads through a hilly region northeast of Funchal, with municipal bus connections to its start and finish. Close to two hours are required to walk from Curral dos Romeiros, east of Monte, along the Levada dos Tornis, lined with lilies of the valley, to São João de Latrão, or, a little further, to Palheiro Ferreiro. The indefatigable hiker may wish to extend the itinerary from Monte as far as Camacha, a trek lasting some five hours. Curral dos Romeiros to São João de Latrão is one section of this longer trail.

! *Baedeker* TIP

Amigos da Natureza

The »Amigos da Natureza«, the »Nature Friends« of Madeira, regularly go on challenging hikes. Guests are welcome and are not charged (Information: Virgilio Hobrega, Tel: 291 236 881 (home) und 291 237 627 (work).

From Pico do Arieiro to Pico Ruivo

A most rewarding, if challenging, hike through the island's highest inland region. Around four hours in duration, it crosses the mountains from Pico do Arieiro to Pico Ruivo. The trail is signposted but not very secure in places. The height difference during the course of this walk is approx. 900m/ 2950ft. As there are no bus services to Pico do Arieiro, a car or taxi is needed to reach the point of departure. Before setting out, be sure to check the weather forecast and that the path is actually free, as landslides occur from time to time.

From Camacha to Santo da Serra

Beginning in Camacha and ending in Sítio das Quatro Estradas, both of which can easily be reached by bus from Funchal, this is a popular hike and not too difficult. The buses run fairly infrequently, so it is worth examining the timetables in advance. Moving through an attractive terraced landscape, the walk offers a host of beautiful views towards the east of the island. The path rises and falls some 150m/500ft, takes around four and a half hours, and is not recommended for vertigo sufferers!

From Ribeiro Frio to Portela

Approx. 10km/6mi in length, this rather more testing hike along the Levada do Furado and Levada da Portela takes close to three and a half hours and is one of the most commonly recommended levada walks, listed in almost every guide book. It shows to advantage Madeira's vegetation in the higher, more remote parts of the island. The path makes its way along a northern slope at an altitude of around 800m/2600ft and into a – mostly shaded – evergreen laurel forest with countless species of moss, fern and lichen. A warm pullover will be of more use than sun protection.

Ponta do Pargo circuit

A three and a half hour hike with splendid scenery in the westernmost part of Madeira. Best approached by car, the circuit begins and ends at the church of Ponta do Pargo. With a height difference of around 200m/650ft, the light and friendly terrain is dotted with small woods and fern slopes which provide far-reaching views out to sea.

On the Paúl da Serra plateau

This hike across the plateau promises fantastic scenery and a succession of marvellous views of the south coast below. There are no particular obstructions or difficult climbs, but at one point it is necessary to cross a narrow watercourse via stepping stones. Sun protection is advised, as there is no shade along the path. The Levada do Paúl ends in a retention pond which supplies the hydroelectric power station at Calheta. The walk begins in the car park by the Cristo Rei statue in a sharp bend of the 209 and ends about an hour and a half later at the car park alongside the Nossa Senhora de Fátima chapel.

Sights from A to Z

OUTSTANDING NATURAL
BEAUTY AND MUCH MORE
TO DISCOVER ON THE
»GREEN PEARL IN
THE OCEAN« – GET TO KNOW
THE FINEST PLACES ON THIS
ISLAND OF FLOWERS

✳ Calheta

C 2

Altitude: 0 – 230m/754ft   **Population:** approx. 5500

In former times Calheta was the centre of sugar cane cultivation on Madeira. Little evidence remains, with the exception of the Moinho de Açúcar, a dilapidated sugar mill at the beach, and a working distillery which still produces the aguardente sugarcane spirit.

Calheta lies in southwest Madeira, with a good road connection to Funchal, namely the 101. Approaching from Funchal, but avoiding the new tunnel, a **bathing area** greets visitors at the entrance to the parish, with a breakwater keeping out the Atlantic waves to ensure calm waters for swimmers. To the east lies an **artificial beach** with imported Moroccan sand. A marina has also been established.

History   Calheta is verifiably one of the **oldest settlements** on Madeira, receiving its town charter as early as 1502. João Gonçalves Zarco, the man who discovered Madeira, is said to have given large areas of cultivable land to his children here. Calheta later had its own customs post for sugar exports from Madeira. When the fortunes of the Madeiran sugar industry experienced a downturn, Calheta's importance waned.

The fine sandy beach was artificially landscaped, breakwaters protecting it from the bigger waves

▶ VISITING CALHETA

WHERE TO EAT

▶ Moderate

Engenho Velho
Quinta do Ledo, Arco de Calheta
Tel. 291 820 500
Typical Madeiran dishes with a surprisingly different touch – perhaps as a result of the experience the host Leopoldo Gonçalves gleaned from his time with the family in Brazil.

Restaurante Madalena do Mar
Sítio da Vargem, Av. 1° Fevereiro 114
Madalena do Mar

Tel. 291 972 081
Large, bustling restaurant, with seafood and fish prominent on the menu.

WHERE TO STAY

▶ Budget

Hotel Calheta Beach
Vila
Tel. 291 820 300
Fax 291 820 301
www.galoresort.com
Fitness, health and sport are high on the agenda here.

What to See in Calheta

Regrettably, the parish church of Calheta is usually closed. The oldest parts were erected as long ago as 1430, and extensive rebuilding took place in 1639, Those lucky enough to find it open will be able to admire the **Mudéjar wooden ceiling** of the chancel, one of the finest examples to have survived on Madeira of this style, which developed in Spain (► Arts and Culture p. 43). Well worth seeing is an ebony and silver tabernacle donated by King Manuel I.

✳
Parish church

Alongside the church, the old **sugar factory** with equipment and machinery can be visited. At harvest time in April and May, the factory is in operation and its **rum, aguardente and sugar syrup** products can be sampled and purchased in the small tasting room. The second sugar mill at the beach is nothing more than a ruin, its rusty machines gathered together as a kind of open-air museum.

> **!** *Baedeker* TIP
>
> ### Art in Calheta
> In Calheta's Centro das Artes/Casa das Mudas, the architecture of the building deserves note. Temporary exhibitions of art are held inside (opening hours: daily except Mon 10am – 7pm)

Around Calheta

With a little good fortune, a trip to the Capela dos Reis Magos (Chapel of the Three Kings), in the midst of the fields of Lombo dos Reis, a district of the somewhat sprawling parish of Estreito da Calheta above Calheta itself, can be quite a treat. Unfortunately, the

Capela dos Reis Magos

chapel is usually closed. The restored interior of the small church is one of the finest examples of Manueline architecture on Madeira.

Madalena do Mar The little village of Madalena do Mar can lay claim to **historical significance** on the grounds that it was said to have been founded by Vladislaus III of Poland in the year 1457. Official records state that Vladislaus III, King of Poland, was killed in the Battle of Varna in 1444, a crushing defeat at the hands of the Turks. According to legend, however, he survived the carnage and lived on under a different name. His vow to undertake a pilgrimage brought him to Madeira, where João Gonçalves Zarco gave him extensive latifundia, including the place known today as Madalena do Mar. In the dark as to his origins, the locals dubbed him **Henrique Alemão** (Henry the German). He is said to lie buried in the crypt of the small village church of Santa Catarina.

Modern pool ▶ Madalena's swimming facilities at the western edge of the village, just before the tunnel, have been given a facelift with new snack bars and a concrete sunbathing zone.

✳ Camacha

C 6

Altitude: approx. 715m/2345ft   **Population:** approx. 6300

Camacha, in the eastern part of Madeira, is renowned as a centre of basketry, hence the procession of bus tours which include it on their island itineraries.

Home of basketry Almost every one of the 6300 inhabitants has some involvement in this craft, which has been a feature of Madeiran life since the 16th century but really came into its own through the efforts of English traders who settled on the island in the 19th century. The bulk of basketware production is arduous, poorly paid home labour.

▶ VISITING CAMACHA

WHERE TO EAT
▶ **Inexpensive**
O Relógio
At Café Relógio
Tel. 291 922 777
Large restaurant, catering primarily to coach trips, with a marvellous panorama across the valley. Folklore performances on many evenings.

WHERE TO STAY
▶ **Mid-range**
Estalagem Relógio
In the Café Relógio building
Tel. 291 922 777
Fax 291 922 415
24 rooms
Modern, comfortable establishment, with good-class furnishings.

Artisans at work can be seen in Café Relógio

What to See in Camacha

The simple houses on Largo da Achada, the village square at the centre of Camacha, are unremarkable. A commemorative plaque in the centre of the square recalls a football game played on Madeira in 1875 which went down in history as **the first-ever football match in Portugal**. Harry Hinton was the Englishman responsible for beginning the great tradition of Portuguese football.

Centre

The famous Café Relógio, with its unusual clock tower, is situated on the village square and was once the imposing residence of a British merchant family. Today it houses the salesrooms of **Madeira's largest exporter of wickerwork**, shipping its products all over the world. Visitors can see how baskets, chairs or complete suites of furniture being weaved. An entire zoo of wickerwork animals is also on display ☉ (opening hours: 9am – 6pm daily, demonstration workshop only Mon – Sat).

Café Relógio

There is a viewing point alongside Café Relógio, looking towards the south coast and Ilhas Desertas – spoilt somewhat by the road which now runs in front of it.

◄ Viewing point

On the opposite side of the village square, the Casa do Povo (house of the people) is home to an exhibition on **life in the Camacha region**, mainly featuring basketry (Casa do Povo da Camacha, Sítio da Igreja, tel. 291 922 118).

Casa Etnográfica da Camacha

✶ Câmara de Lobos

D 5

Altitude: 0 – 205m/672ft   **Population:** approx. 5000

One of the most famous visitors to Câmara de Lobos was Winston Churchill, who was so enamoured of the scenery that he painted a number of landscapes.

Bay of wolves   The fishing village of Câmara de Lobos owes its name to the seals (Portuguese: »lobos marinhos« = sea wolves), specifically the monk seals (▶ Baedeker Special, p. 120) which once populated the bay. Founded by João Gonçalves Zarco as long ago as 1420, it was only upgraded to town and city status in 1996. Câmara de Lobos is the **focal point of the island's fishing industry**, with the black scabbard fish (▶ p. 24) in particular being caught at depths of 800m/2600ft and more in the night. The vines above the town are some of the finest on the island. Whilst the men are employed either in fishery or in the vineyards, many of the womenfolk work from home as embroiderers. The overall impression is of poverty, with social tension as obvious to visitors as to the locals. Câmara de Lobos is renowned for a nicely mixed poncha (▶Practicalities: Food and Drink p. 74).

> **? DID YOU KNOW ...?**
>
> ■ ... that around 700 fishermen and some 440 boats are officially registered on Madeira? Numbers are declining, however; before the turn of the millennium, twice as many men set out from the island to the Atlantic fishing grounds.

▶ VISITING CÂMARA DE LOBOS

INFORMATION
Largo da República (in the town hall)
Tel. 291 943 470

WHERE TO EAT
▶ Moderate
As Vides
Igreja, Estreito de Câmara de Lobos
Tel. 291 945 322
Traditional restaurant and the first on Madeira to serve beef on laurel-wood skewers.

▶ Inexpensive
Churchill's
Rua João Gonçalves, 39
Tel. 291 941 451
Churchill dined and painted here; good, well-known restaurant. Popular dish: tasty grilled fish with salad.

WHERE TO STAY
▶ Mid-range
Estalagem Quinta do Estreito
Tel. 291 775 936, fax 291 762 171
www.quintadoestreitomadeira.com
Old country residence in the mountains above Câmara de Lobos. 44 rooms, 2 suites, restaurant, swimming pool with pleasant relaxation zone. Bus shuttle to Funchal runs twice daily.

What to See in Câmara de Lobos

The friendly **old town**, graced with winding alleys and little squares, stretches across a long ridge known as the Ilhéu (small island). Beneath the Ilhéu, a promenade runs along the seafront.

There are many colourful fishing boats down in the **harbour**, still built in traditional fashion at the small wharf. It was here that a replica of the Santa Maria, the ship with which Columbus sailed the seas, was constructed for the EXPO 1998 in Lisbon. The best views of the charming harbour bay can be enjoyed from above the wharf, where **Winston Churchill** once sat and painted; the spot is marked by a memorial plaque. A new pool complex (Piscinas das Salinas) and

Churchill enjoyed this view

attractive promenade now occupy the site where fishermen laid out their catch to dry in years gone by. Largo da República has also been redesigned.

The chapel of Nossa Senhora da Conceição at the harbour is nothing special to look at from the outside. It was constructed in 1702 on the site of the first chapel erected on the island by Zarco. The beautiful altar with richly gilded wood carvings is most impressive.

Capela Nossa Senhora da Conceição

Not far from the harbour, the **market hall**, though smaller than the one in Funchal, is well worth a look.

Higher up in the western part of the old town, on the almost circular Largo da República, stands the **parish church of São Sebastião**, some elements of which date back to

> **! Baedeker TIP**
>
> **Fine wines**
>
> Henriques & Henriques is one of the best addresses for fine Madeira wines, rum and liqueurs. The quality of their products can be put to the test in the tasting room (signposted from Largo da República; Mon – Fri 9am – noon and 3pm – 6pm, mornings only on Saturdays).

around 1430, making it one of the oldest chapels on the island. It was remodelled in Baroque style in the 18th century and decorated with splendid wood carvings, some in gold. Its walls are adorned with artistic azulejo pictures.

RESCUE IN SIGHT? A NEW GENERATION OF MONK SEAL CUBS

In 1419, in a bay of Madeira, the first settlers happened upon thousands of monk seals – »lobos marinhos« in Portuguese. They named this stretch of coast »Câmara do Lobos«. 500 years on, the scene has changed completely.

The monk seal is under threat of extinction, not only on the Madeiran archipelago but the world over. In 1990 the regional government of Madeira took action to save its last ten or so monk seals. And in late 2001, there was good news from the Ilhas Desertas: the birth of **three monk seal babies**, weighing between 15kg and 25kg (33lb to 55lb) and measuring 80–90cm/31–35 inches. This suggests grounds for optimism that the Madeiran population, now numbering around 30, will indeed survive.

At great risk

Altogether, of the around 5000 animals that made up the monk seal population of the Mediterranean and near Atlantic waters just a few decades ago, a mere 300 have survived. Slaughtered in former times for their **blubber, meat and skin**, which was cured for leather, some seal products had rather dubious uses: sealskin shoes were said to help against gout, the right flipper of a monk seal under the pillow was thought to alleviate insomnia, and a sealskin tent was believed to protect its occupants against lightning strikes. In spite of this, the seal population was never dangerously low – the threat came later, from pollution on the one hand and intensive fishing on the other. Fishermen still see seals as competitors that eat their potential catch and destroy their nets. The seals die in nets intended not for them but for fish, whilst overfishing decimates their own food supply: seals have been found to have died of osteoporosis and undernourishment in the Mediterranean.

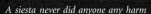

A siesta never did anyone any harm

The »monk«

The Mediterranean monk seal is of medium size. It can live for up to 40 years of age and a fully-grown adult can weigh up to 400kg/880lb, measuring up to 3m/10ft. There are **three explanations for the name**: the upper side of their body is brown, like that of a monk's cowl. The males develop a noticeable layer of blubber around their necks, a real double chin. When they straighten up, the folds of skin resemble the habit of a Franciscan monk. And finally, unlike many other breeds of seal, monk seals do not travel far, preferring to live like eremitic monks in remote, inaccessible places, seeking peace and refuge in caves or grottoes.

The human problem

The monk seal's fatal attachment to its place of origin makes it particularly vulnerable to human interference. **Construction work along the coast** and an **increase in leisure activities in the water** have left monk seals with few undisturbed spots in which to rear their young. Even chance encounters with swimmers, surfers or divers can quickly lead to seals abandoning their offspring, who prove incapable of fending for themselves – another fundamental reason for the dwindling numbers of monk seals.

Protection zones

In order to protect and develop the existing colony, the regional government of Madeira established a nature reserve on the **Ilhas Desertas** in 1990. A strict watch is kept over the islands, with access restricted to authorized scientists. To prevent monk seals facing a miserable death by getting trapped in nets, all coastal areas have been cleared of old gillnets and new ones are forbidden. For some time now, plans to establish another small monk seal colony on Ponta de São Lourenço have been underway.

There is not much to do in the harbour of Câmara de Lobos. Plenty of time for a game of cards

Around Câmara de Lobos

✱
Pico da Torre

There are specially fine views of the town and harbour bay from the Pico da Torre viewing point (205m/672ft), above the town to the northeast.

Estreito de Câmara de Lobos

Estreito de Câmara de Lobos lies above Câmara de Lobos at approx. 500m/1640ft and is best known for its excellent wine. Every autumn, the grape harvest is celebrated in a **wine festival lasting several days**. Its wine tastings and folklore performances have seen the event develop into a real tourist attraction. The **Sunday market** in the town centre, attended by many Madeirans, is well worth inspecting.

Quinta Jardim da Serra

A minor road leads north from Estreito de Câmara de Lobos, reaching Quinta Jardim da Serra (750m/2460ft) after 4km/2.5mi for excellent views and good hiking terrain.

✱ ✱ Cabo Girão

One of Europe's highest cliffs

Around 4km beyond Estreito de Câmara de Lobos, a road branches off left to a lookout point across the Cabo Girão. Rising to a height of 580m/1900ft, the cliff face which plummets down to the coast is one of the highest of its kind in Europe – some say, one of the highest in the world. On a clear day there are dizzying views of the small, in some cases tiny, terraced fields far below the cliff. To the east lie

Hold on tight! To look down from almost 600m/1950ft on Cabo Girão, you need a good head for heights

the foothills of Funchal and Câmara de Lobos. On the car park, a tourist information office and a **photography gallery** with interesting historical images of Madeira are open during the high season. In the immediate vicinity of Cabo Girão, a new **cable car**, originally built to transport labourers, connects Rancho with the fields along the coast (the trip costs approx. 5 €). Further inland, the church of Nossa Senhora de Fátima was erected in 1931 and, like the great pilgrimage church on the Portuguese mainland, has a vast square in front of it for assemblies of the faithful.

There are two ways to reach the beach and houses of **Fajã dos Padres**, west of Cabo Girão: by boat or by means of the elevator built into the steep rock face. **Boat or elevator**

Caniçal

Altitude: 0 – 50m/164ft   **Population:** approx. 2000

The history of the village of Caniçal on the east coast of Madeira is inextricably linked to that of whaling. Today, the fishermen fill their nets with tuna.

◉ VISITING CANIÇAL

WHERE TO EAT

► Expensive
O Jardim
Palmeira de Baixo
Tel. 291 969 120
Chef's specials are »bacalhau com natas« (cod with cream) and seafood rice.

► Inexpensive
Amarelo
at the old harbour
Tel. 291 961 798
Locals and tourists alike gather here for a tasty fish stew (caldeirada; advance booking required).

Village of whalers Following massive international protests, whaling ceased here in 1981, where previously 300 whales had been caught and processed per year. A good 200,000 sq km/77,000 sq mi of ocean have now been designated as a marine national park. In order to develop the economy of this barren region after 1981, the government established a free trade zone with a commercial harbour on the site of the earlier whaling station. A large new wharf (for repairs) and an extensive pool complex at the western end of the promenade were also constructed.

What to See in Caniçal

Museu da Baleia (Whale Museum) Since 1990, the small museum has kept alive the past with an array of documents, photographs and whalebone carvings. A **13m/42ft-long replica of a pot whale** is particularly impressive; the whaling boat alongside it underlines the difference in size. An entertaining film documents the efforts of the Madeiran government with regard to nature conservation and environmental protection (opening hours: Tue–Sun 10am–noon and 1pm–6pm).

East of Caniçal, the **Capela da Senhora da Piedade** stands atop a volcanic rock. Every third weekend in September an impressive **water procession** starts here. A small statue of the Virgin Mary (16th century), probably by a Flemish master, is carried from the chapel to Caniçal along the coast in a colourful procession of boats and back to the chapel.

Prainha beach At the foot of the chapel rock is the diminutive beach of Prainha, which enjoys great popularity with local bathers as the **only natural sandy beach** on Madeira.

Caniço

D 6/7

Altitude: 25 – 200m/80 – 650ft   **Population:** approx. 8000

Apart from tourism, the main source of income for the local inhabitants is fruit and vegetable cultivation, hence the proliferation of greenhouses in the area.

The small town of Caniço is situated either side of the river of the same name, just a few miles east of Funchal on the R 101. This narrow watercourse once played an important role: **it was the line between the two administrative regions** into which Madeira was divided. Caniço thus had two parishes and two churches: the church of the Holy Ghost on the left bank and one dedicated to San Antonio on the right. **Two parishes**

What to See in Caniço

The village square, beautifully paved with basalt mosaic stones, is a meeting point for the local people. Here stands the **parish church**, with a dedication inscribed above the portal to the Holy Ghost and San Antonio – although the parishes were united as long ago as the 15th century, the ruinous churches were only torn down and the present structure erected in the 18th century. Also on the village square is the 16th-century **Manueline chapel** of Madre de Deus. **Village square**

One of Madeira's most beautiful steeples can be seen in Caniço

► VISITING CANIÇO

INFORMATION
Caniço de Baixo
Tel. 291 932 919

WHERE TO EAT
► Expensive
O Rústico
Caniço de Baixo
Tel. 291 934 316
The attractive terrace affords the opportunity to enjoy quality Madeiran dishes and marvellous panoramic views. Be sure to sample the home-made sausage.

Baedeker recommendation

► Moderate
A Lareira
Sítio da Vargem
Tel. 291 934 494
Typical regional dishes, fish – including black scabbard fish with banana and almonds – and good soups.

GOING OUT
The Habeas Corpus pub in Caniço de Baixo is open until 2am every night of the week.

✳ Quinta Splendida

At the southern edge of the village lie the grounds of the Quinta Splendida estate. A country residence which has been tastefully converted into a hotel, it is furnished with a wealth of antiques and houses a **gourmet restaurant**. The marvellous landscaped park is well worth a visit.

Caniço de Baixo

Approximately 3km/2mi below Caniço, Caniço de Baixo has developed into Madeira's most important tourist centre alongside Funchal, with an infrastructure to match yet without seeming overrun. Set into the rock, the **seawater bathing pools** of Rocamar and Galomar are suitable for diving and are open to the public as well as hotel guests. Another place to go swimming is the pebble beach of Reis Magos, on the eastern perimeter of the village, as the presence of many Madeirans testifies.

Ponta do Garajau

Leaving Caniço in a southwesterly direction, a road winds its way down to Ponta do Garajau and a huge **statue of Christ**, built in 1927. From the terrace in front, there are far-reaching views across to the bay of Funchal.

Marine national park

The sea beyond Ponta do Garajau, between Ponta da Oliveira (in the east) and São Gonçalo (in the west) is an environmentally protected area called the Reserva Natural Parcial do Garajau. This **paradise for divers** is also populated by groupers, and the sight of an elegant manta gliding through the water is not unusual, particularly in late summer.

Curral das Freiras

✶✶

C 5

Altitude: 690–990m/2260–3248ft   **Population:** approx. 1500

Curral das Freiras – literally »Valley of the Nuns« – is one of Madeira's most impressive landscapes. The most commanding view of this scenery can be enjoyed when approaching from Eira do Serrado.

Both the valley and the village were given their name by the **nuns of the Santa Clara convent in Funchal**, who retreated here in 1566 following an attack by French corsairs. In earlier times, the almost circular Curral das Freiras was thought to be an extinct volcanic crater. More recent research suggests it is merely a product of erosion: the river which now runs through the valley has taken the soft tuff with it through the ages, whilst the harder basalt of the steep rock face remains.

Valley of the Nuns

Passing through the eucalyptus forest, dense in places, on the way from Funchal to Curral das Freiras, Eira do Serrado is reached (Serrado saddle; 1026m/3366ft) at the northeastern edge of the Pico do Serrado. Along the way, a road branches off to the right to a mountain hotel (1km/half a mile), where the car park leads to a pleasant, shady forest trail and on to a panoramic platform, high above the Curral valley. Visitors can gaze **from a dizzying height** into the deep basin below. Those with enough stamina and a good head for heights can follow a trail down to Curral das Freiras that takes around one and a half hours. A bus leaves from the village church if the journey back up proves a little daunting.

✶✶
The view from Eira do Serrado

The valley of Curral das Freiras was already cultivated by nuns of the Santa Clara convent before the corsairs' attack in 1566, but the village was only established some 200 years later. In the 19th century, nuns had the

The vertiginous view of Curral das Freiras from the Eira do Serrado

VISITING CURRAL DAS FREIRAS

WHERE TO EAT AND STAY
▶ Budget
Estalagem Eira do Serrado
Panoramic view at Eira do Serrado
Tel. 291 710 060, fax 291 710 061
www.eiradoserrado.com; 25 Z.
Isolated, comfortable mountain hotel
and restaurant; at the heart of a mar-
vellous natural landscape, tranquillity

is guaranteed in the evening and
throughout the night, whilst tourist
buses roll in by day.

EVENTS
Specialities are worth celebrating: for
the chestnuts of Curral das Freiras,
there is an annual event on 1 November.

church of Nossa Senhora do Livramento built at the southern edge
of the village centre. The **magnificent landscape as seen from the
village** is certain to impress. In addition to grain, wine and fruit, especially chestnuts, tourism plays an increasing role. Souvenir shops
and cafés are clustered around the village square.

Faial

B 6

Altitude: approx. 150m/490ft   **Population:** approx. 1500

**The pretty little town of Faial lies high above the northeast coast
amidst fertile fruit and vegetable gardens. Wine growing is also of
economic importance. This region's rural prosperity is manifested
in the well-kept houses of Faial.**

 VISITING FAIAL

WHERE TO EAT
▶ Moderate
Grutas do Faial
Lombo de Baixo
Tel. 291 572 817
Typical and delicious island dishes.

*Esplanada Praça
do Engenho*
Rua da Praia
Porto da Cruz
Tel. 291 563 680

Simple, typical fare, including good
fish dishes.

WHERE TO STAY
▶ Budget
Hotel Albergaria do Penedo
Rua Dr. João Abel de Freitas, 23–25
Porto da Cruz
Tel. 291 563 011
Fax 291 563 012; 8 Z.
Small hotel right at the harbour, good
and simple.

A striking rock formation – Eagle Rock at Faial. In the distance, the eastern peninsula of Madeira

What to See in and Around Faial

Eagle Rock

The church vestibule provides lovely views of Madeira's northern coast, with Faial's own landmark, Eagle Rock (Penha de Águia, 594m/1948ft), an isolated, almost **cubic cliff towering into the sky**. The name is a reference to the ospreys who nest in its heights. For a time, they were thought to have died out on Madeira, but happily they have been sighted again more recently.

Swim and splash

Praia do Faial, an artificial **lagoon** at the mouth of the Ribeira São Roque do Faial, attracts swimmers with on-site changing rooms, a children's playground and deck chairs for rent.

Fortim do Faial

Fortim do Faial is a treasure on the road to Santana, a defence post against pirates in the 18th century, equipped with ten English cannon. Old photographs and etchings in the small fort recall the island in former times.

Porto da Cruz

Porto da Cruz – east of Faial, on the coast beyond Eagle Rock – is an attractive little place with a **seawater swimming pool** down in the bay. Higher up, next to the church, is a panoramic terrace with beautiful views of the bay, the remains of an old fort on the rocks jutting out from the coast and a sugar factory chimney – Porto da Cruz was, for many years, a **centre of sugarcane cultivation**.

✦✦ Funchal

D 5/6

Altitude: 0 – 550m/1800ft   **Population:** approx. 130,000

The houses of the picturesquely situated capital city of Funchal line the slopes of a mountain range which rises to some 1200m/3900ft, lending it the appearance of an amphitheatre. A stroll through the streets of the old town or along the harbour can be as rewarding as a visit to the city's churches, palaces and museums, whilst the rich subtropical vegetation found in splendid gardens is truly something to behold. Funchal owes its name to the wild fennel (funcho in Portuguese) which covered the bay at the time of the island's discovery.

Vibrant centre Funchal and its surrounding area are the vibrant centre of the island, home to around half the people of Madeira. The city is the administrative centre of the Região Autónoma da Madeira, a trade and banking centre, the seat of a Roman Catholic bishop and a university city. The archipelago's only sizeable harbour is here – once an important hub for international transatlantic shipping, it is now primarily frequented by cruise ships.

Madeira's capital stretches across the entire bay and up the hillside

GRAND CAFE

... *and a table outside is not bad either*

VISITING FUNCHAL

INFORMATION

*Direcção Regional do Turismo –
Região Autónoma da Madeira*
Avenida M. Arriaga, 18
P-9004-519 Funchal
Tel. 291 211 900
Fax 291 232 151
www.madeiratourism.org

Avenida M. Arriaga, 16
Tel. 291 211 902

Estrada Monumental (Lido)
Tel. 291 775 254

TRANSPORT

Driving a car is not a pleasurable
experience during rush hour, and
parking spaces are scarce. From Funchal's hotel zone it is advisable to use a
hotel shuttle or one of the orange
municipal buses (a 7-day ticket is good
value for money) to reach the town
and negotiate the centre on foot.
Bearing in mind the frequently uneven
and slippery cobblestones, sturdy
footwear comes in handy! Most bus
services stop at the harbour on
Avenida do Mar, a convenient starting
point for a round trip.

SIGHTSEEING

An open-top bus leaves on the hour
throughout the day (Mar – Oct) or
every 90 minutes off-season (Nov –
Feb) to guide visitors through Funchal
with an English commentary; tours
depart from Avenida do Mar at the
harbour.

CAFES

Grand Café Golden Gate
Av. Arriaga / Av. Zarco
A hint of central European coffee-
house atmosphere ...

Café do Teatro
Avenida Arriaga
A decidedly elegant café and bar inside
the theatre; lovely courtyard

WHERE TO EAT
▶ Expensive
① *Casa Velha*
Rua Imperatriz D. Amélia, 69
Tel. 291 205 600
Fine restaurant, renowned for its fish
dishes and wine list

② *Casa Madeirense*
Estrada Monumental, 153
Tel. 291 766 700
Rustic interior and very good cuisine.
Specialities: cataplana with seafood
and fish, lobster, flambéed meat in
wine and garlic sauce, unusual appe-
tizers

③ *Quinta Palmeira*
Avenida do Infante, 17-19
Tel. 291 221 814
Taken over by Manuel de Sousa in
1982 and famous for impeccable
service, excellent food and a wine list
for the discerning

▶ Moderate

④ *Café do Museu*
Praça do Município
Tel. 291 281 121
Popular lunchtime meeting place,
friendly service. Excellent tuna car-
paccio and vegetarian lasagne

Luxury and nostalgia: Reid's Palace Hotel

⑤ *Combatentes*
Rua Ivens / Rua de S. Francisco
Tel. 291 221 388
Neat little municipal restaurant at the
Jardim Municipal, serving good re-
gional and international dishes

⑥ *Doca do Cavacas*
Rua Ponta da Cruz
Sítio Piornais São Martinho
Tel. 291 762 057
Local Madeirans are also happy to
make the trip out of town to savour
the fine fish dishes in this restaurant

⑦ *Escola Profissional de Hoteleria*
Trav. do Piornais, São Martinho
Tel. 291 764 393, 291 764 403
Varying menus created by students of
the prestigious school of hotel man-
agement – often a pleasant surprise for
relatively little money. Transfers possible

▶ Inexpensive

⑧ *Londres*
Rua Carreira, 64
Tel. 291 235 329
Large portions, typically hearty fare,
also popular with the locals

⑨ *O Almirante*
Largo do Poço, 1–2
Tel. 291 224 252
Good regional cuisine served here

WHERE TO STAY

▶ Luxury

① *Reid's Palace Hotel*
Estrada Monumental, 139
Tel. 291 717 171, fax 291 717 164
www.reidspalace.com; 169 rooms
For a good 115 years, the legendary
Reid's has been the finest place to stay
on Madeira

② *Hotel Pestana Casino Park*
Rua Imperatriz D. Amélia, 55
Tel. 291 209 100, fax 291 232 076
www.pestana.com; 373 rooms
Crafted in concrete by the Brazilian
architect Oscar Niemeyer, this is one
of the best addresses on Madeira.
Spacious rooms, many with a sea view;
wide range of entertainment and
sporting activities on offer

③ *Estalagem Quinta da Bela Vista*
Caminho do Avista Navios, 4
Tel. 291 706 401, fax 291 706 411
www.belavistamadeira.com; 89 rooms
A family-owned, modernized quinta,
situated above the town with views of
the mountains and the sea

▶ Mid-range

④ *Quinta Perestrello*
Rua Dr. Pita, 3
Tel. 291 706 700, fax 291 706 706
www.charminghotelsmadeira.com
Stylish hotel with 37 rooms in a 150-
year-old house with a modern annex

⑤ *Madeira Regency Cliff*
Travessa da Quinta Calaça, 6
Tel. 291 710 700, fax 291 710 701
www.regency-hotels-resorts.com
Modern style hotel with 60 rooms,
directly overlooking the sea. Lovely
breakfast and restaurant terrace. Large
seawater swimming pool, open to the
public, below the hotel

⑥ *Hotel Madeira Panorâmico*
Rua Estados Unidos da América, 34
Tel. 291 766 113, fax 291 766 114
www.madeira-panoramico.com; 81
rooms
Modern hotel to the west of the town.
The more expensive rooms boast
fantastic views across the bay of
Funchal!

► **Budget**
⑦ *Mimosa Hotel • Estrelícia Hotel*
Mimosa: Rua da Casa Blanca
Tel. 291 706 621, fax 291 764 859
Estrelícia: Caminho Velho da Ajuda
Tel. 291 706 660, fax 291 764 859
www.dorisol.pt; 348 rooms in total
Two mid-range hotels in one, each
with a swimming pool and snack bar,
restaurant and night club. Functional
rooms, some with kitchenette

⑧ *Pensião Vila Teresinha*
Rua das Cruzes, 21
Tel. 291 741 723
Fax 291 744 515; 12 rooms
www.vilateresinha.com
Simple, pleasantly appointed guest-
house close to the Quinta das Cruzes
with a beautiful rooftop terrace

WHERE TO GO OUT

Young folk go clubbing after midnight
at Vespas, whilst their elders are more
likely to be found in the O Farol
(Hotel Pestana Carlton Madeira) disco
on a Friday or Saturday night from
11pm, or in the Copacabana nightclub

at the casino. Jazz fans can enjoy live
music at Jam – Jazz & Music Lounge
or in the Moonlight Bar of the Tivoli
Ocean Park hotel.

EVENTS AND FESTIVALS

April's Festa da Flôr is a wonderful
flower festival, welcoming springtime.
In June, the Festival do Atlântico
features classical concerts and ballet,
along with folklore events.

Springtime splashes of colour at the flower festival

SHOPPING

The old town of Funchal provides a
wide range of shopping, from international chains to bric-a-brac stores.
North of the cathedral, the shop-lined
Rua do Aljube leads to the Bazar do
Povo department store, which was
founded in 1883. Rua Dr. Fernão
Ornelas, west of the market hall, is
another of the most important shopping streets. There are several malls to
wander through, such as the Marina
Shopping Center at the harbour, the
Eden Mar and the Monumental Lido
in the hotel zone above the lido or, far
to the southwest, the Centromar.

Funchal Map

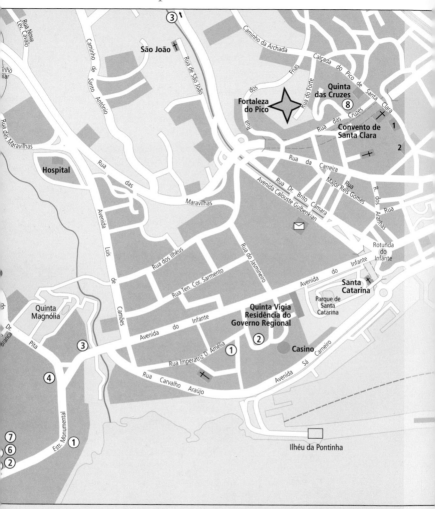

1 Museu Frederico de Freitas
2 Museu Municipal
3 Museu Photographia Vicentes
4 Câmara Municipal
5 Museu de Arte Sacra
6 Madeira Wine Company
7 Teatro Municipal
8 Alfândega Velha
9 Centro Museológico do Açúcar
10 IBTAM

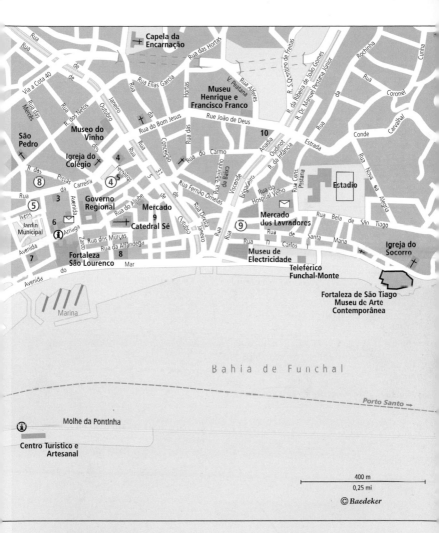

Bahia de Funchal

Porto Santo →

Molhe da Pontinha

Centro Turístico e
Artesanal

400 m
0,25 mi

© Baedeker

Where to stay
① Reid's Palace Hotel
② Hotel Pestana Casino Park
③ Estalagem Quinta da Bela Vista
④ Quinta Perestrello
⑤ Madeira Regency Cliff
⑥ Hotel Madeira Panorâmico
⑦ Mimosa Hotel – Estrelícia Hotel
⑧ Pensião Vila Teresinha

Where to eat
① Casa Velha
② Casa Madeirense
③ Quinta Palmeira
④ Café do Museu
⑤ Combatentes
⑥ Doca do Cavacas
⑦ Escola Profissional de Hotelaria
⑧ Londres
⑨ O Almirante

Tourism Tourism is concentrated in the western part of town, where a veritable **hotel zone** has developed, consisting largely of 3-star to 5-star hotels. Funchal is also where Madeira's nightlife plays out: evening entertainments include a casino, cinema and theatre.

1497	Funchal is proclaimed capital of Madeira.
1508	Funchal is given city status.
1513/1514	The first fort is constructed and the cathedral consecrated.
From 1860	Funchal becomes a tourist destination for the wealthy European upper classes.
1891	Reid's Hotel is opened.
1976	Funchal becomes seat of the regional assembly.

History Before people could settle in Funchal, fires were set to clear the bay of fennel. João Gonçalves Zarco was allotted the west of Madeira in 1450 and initially made Câmara de Lobos his base, before later settling in Funchal. The eastern part of Madeira was governed by the administration in Machico. King Manuel I put an end to the partition of the island in 1497, declaring Funchal its capital. The history of Funchal is, by and large, synonymous with that of Madeira, as it profited from the boom in sugar trade and was the chief trading centre for Madeira wine – the city's coat of arms thus shows five sugar loaves and grapes. It did not take long for Funchal to become the **focal point of Madeiran tourism**, as it still is today.

Short trip Any short trip to Funchal should at least take in the area around **Avenida do Mar** and **Avenida Arriaga**, the **cathedral** and the **market hall**. The tourist information office can be found in Avenida Arriaga in the centre.

Between Avenida do Mar and Avenida Arriaga

The harbour is the ideal place to commence a walk through Funchal's centre. Here, where ships bound for Brazil and India came into port in years gone by, **the attractive promenade** Avenida do Mar now extends along the seafront. Vast cruise ships can be seen across the marina. One of the most striking boats is the *Vagrant*, which once belonged to The Beatles and is now a floating restaurant. A row of bars and boat excursion operators await the tourists. Sightseeing tours depart from above the marina.

! *Baedeker* TIP

The Madeira Balloon

Tethered on Avenida do Mar, one of the largest gas balloons in the world elevates visitors some 150m/490ft up in the sky, safely attached to a rope – but at a dizzying price. A small exhibition room in the café next door tells the story of aviation on Madeira.

Highlights Funchal

Cathedral
Its magnificent cedar roof is one of the finest in all Portugal.
► page 139

Mercado dos Lavradores
Fruit and vegetables, fish and cheese as far as the eye can see
► page 144

Cable car to Monte
Splendid panoramic views from the glass cabins of the Teleférico
► page 145, 161

Madeira Wine Company
Everything there is to know about the famous Madeira wine
► page 143

Museum of Sacred Art
What could be purchased with sugar, once upon a time ...
► page 147

Embroidery Museum
The Institute for Embroidery, Tapestry and Handicrafts is home to an impressive collection of Madeiran embroidery.
► page 146

Quinta das Cruzes
The museum offers an insight into the island's cultural history, whilst the splendid garden features attractive examples of stonemasonry and a collection of orchids.
► page 149

Reid's Palace Hotel
Remember to wear a tie for tea at five.
► page 152, 154

Jardim Botânico
Luxuriant tropical and subtropical plants
► page 154

Fortaleza de São Lourenço

Madeira's first fortress, the Fortaleza de São Lourenço, stands on Avenida do Mar. It was built in the 16th century on the site of older, rudimentary defences and has been rebuilt on a number of occasions. Today it serves as residence for the Minister of the Republic, Portugal's representative on Madeira. The mighty 18th-century sea façade of the eastern tower displays the Portuguese emblem with the cross of the Order of the Knights of Christ, the Portuguese successors to the Knights Templar, and two armillary spheres. These nautical devices symbolize Portugal's era of discovery.

Alfândega Velha (Old Customs House)

Further to the east is the Old Customs House (Alfândega Velha). Little remains of the original construction of 1477. Having been almost completely destroyed by an earthquake in 1748, it was rebuilt and extended in the 18th century. The rather unostentatious entrance on the rear side of the building (►p. 49) is considered a **fine specimen of Manueline architecture**.

Cathedral (Sé)

Funchal's cathedral, known as Sé in Portuguese (from the Latin sedes = see, seat), is reached via the pretty pedestrian zone in Rua João Tavira. In 1514 it became the first overseas Portuguese cathedral to be

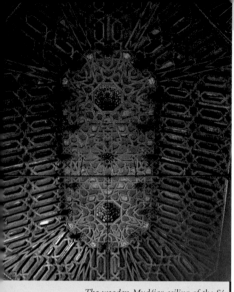

The wooden Mudéjar ceiling of the Sé

consecrated. Its rather plain, almost austere exterior is characterized by the contrast of white plaster and dark basalt. A decorative rosette is emblazoned above the Gothic main portal. Higher up, at the very top is a **cross of the Order of Christ**, of which King Manuel I was Grand Master – this cross is also still an element in the flag of Madeira. The mighty, rectangular main tower is crowned by a pyramidal roof with geometrically arranged tiles.

Inside, the cathedral impresses in many respects: the high altar and the eight side altars of the basilica with its nave and two aisles were brought from Flanders in the 16th century, as were the choir stalls. They were paid for from the proceeds of the sugar trade, so lucrative at the time. Particularly worthy of note is the magnificent **Mudéjar-style ceiling**, artfully carved from Madeira cedarwood. The **keystones in the choir vault**, with the cross of the Order of Christ, the Portuguese crest and the armillary sphere (► Fortaleza de São Lourenço) are quite beautiful (opening hours: 8am – noon and 4pm – 6.30pm).

»The City of Sugar« East of the cathedral lies Praça de Colombo, its centre decorated with a mosaic of the Funchal coat of arms. The Núcleo Museológico »A Cidade do Açucar« shows the most precious **craft artefacts from the heyday of the sugar trade**, namely the 15th and 16th centuries; here it is possible to see what could be purchased with the profits from the sugar boom. Also on display are items excavated from a neighbouring house which once belonged to a Flemish sugar trader in which Columbus is said to have stayed (opening hours: Mon – Fri 10am – 12.30pm and 2pm – 6pm).

Avenida Arriaga West of the cathedral, Avenida Arriaga runs northwards, parallel to Avenida do Mar. This lively street in the town centre, now partly pedestrianized, is awash with vivid blue and violet jacaranda blossoms. At the crossroads with Avenida Zarco, a (1934) monument by Francisco Franco honours the island's discoverer, João Gonçalves Zarco (►Museum, p. 142).

Housed in a former Franciscan monastery opposite the Fortaleza de São Lourenço and next to the tourist information office, the Madeira Wine Company has **the oldest and most important wine cellar on Madeira**. Guided tours explain how Madeira wine is made (groups should book in advance). To round things off in the nicest possible fashion, there are two tasting rooms where the wine may be sampled and, of course, purchased. A small museum displays old letters and documents, along with historical tools (opening hours: Mon – Fri 9.30am – 6pm, reception closed 1pm – 2.30pm, Saturdays 10am – 1pm; guided tours Mon – Sat; individual visitors are advised to check if advance booking is necessary, tel. 291 740 110, fax 291 740 111; www.madeirawinecompany.com).

✶✶
Madeira Wine Company

☉

From the Madeira Wine Company it is not far to the lush tropical plants of the **municipal gardens**, created in 1878 on the site of the monastery gardens. The stone coat of arms of the Franciscan order can be seen in the southeast corner of the grounds. In 1982 a statue of Francis of Assisi was erected in honour of his 800th birthday. A popular photo opportunity is a statue of two boys playing at the duck pond.
Two interesting buildings stand opposite: one is the Chamber of Commerce, embellished with a blue and white, tiled façade depicting **typical motifs of the island**. The other is the **municipal theatre** (Teatro Municipal), established in 1888. As well as plays and films, art exhibitions and concerts are also staged here.

✶
Jardim Municipal

> **!** *Baedeker* TIP
>
> **A snack In the park**
> Somewhat hidden away, towards the back of the Jardim Municipal, a simple kiosk café serves snacks and drinks. Tables and chairs stand in the shade of tall trees.

A little further on, at **Dioqo's Wine Spirits Shop**, books, maps and copperplate engravings concerning Christopher Columbus can be viewed. They were collected from all over the world by the shop's founder and now comprise a small museum (opening hours: Mon – Fri 9.30am – 1pm and 3pm – 7pm, Sat 9.30am – 1pm).

Museu Cristóvão

☉

Avenida Arriaga ends at the **Rotunda do Infante**, named after Henry the Navigator (►Famous People), at whose behest of João Gonçalves Zarco reconnoitred Madeira in 1419. The monument, the work of Francisco Franco, was erected in 1947.

Monument to Henry the Navigator

Eastern City Centre

One of Funchal's most splendid sights is the market hall, named »Mercado dos Lavradores« (peasants' market). The blue and white tiled frescoes at the main entrance portray scenes of market life. Inside, the stalls are packed with an unbelievable **abundance of mar-**

✶✶
Market hall – Mercado dos Lavradores

vellous fruits on two levels around a broad court, its walls similarly adorned with tiled frescoes. The lower level is dedicated to local producers on Friday and Saturday mornings. In the eastern section, the fish market building in characteristic 1930s design is above all devoted to delicious tuna and scabbard fish (opening hours: Mon – Fri 8am – 8pm, Sat 7am – 2pm).

South of the market hall, towards the sea, the Praça da Autonomia **monument commemorates the Carnation Revolution of 1974** and the successful attainment of independence for Madeira. At the eastern edge stands the highly interesting **Museu da Electricidade**, offering an excellent insight into the development of electricity on Madeira. A splendid model of the island graphically illustrates by means of small lamps how illumination progressed from 1897 to 1997 (opening hours: 10am – 12.30pm and 2pm – 6pm, daily).

Praça da Autonomia

Immediately to the southeast of the market hall, the Old Town of Funchal begins, once a **district of fishermen and artisans**. Some of its small shops and narrow alleyways still leave a rather humble impression. Attempts are being made to improve the local infrastructure with the help of public investment. There is a small area geared to tourists with a few restaurants. Right in the south is the valley station of the Teleférico, the cable car to Monte.
A worthy addition to the Praça Almirante Reis is the new Madeira Story Centre. This themed centre in the former Santa Maria cinema and erstwhile storehouse of the agricultural society takes visitors on a virtual journey to Madeira's past and its development up to the present day (opening hours: 9am – 8pm daily, except for 25 December).

★ Zona Velha (Old Town)

◄ Teleférico

◄ Madeira Story Centre

At the eastern border of the Zona Velha, the picturesque Fortaleza de São Tiago stands watch over the small harbour bay of the former fishing district. Work began on the site in 1614, with considerable extensions added in 1767. A small military exhibition is joined by the **Museu de Arte Contemporânea** (Museum for Contemporary Art), which shows changing exhibitions of Portuguese painters since around 1960 and a permanent collection of works by the artist Lourdes de Castro (opening hours: Mon – Sat 10am – 12.30pm and 2pm – 5.30pm).

★ Fortaleza de São Tiago

A short distance behind the Fortaleza de São Tiago stands the Igreja do Socorro (Church of the Redeemer), also known as Santa Maria Maior, the parish church of the Old Town. Originally built in the 16th century, the church was dedicated to Saint James the Younger, the patron saint of Funchal, who, according to legend, saved the town from the plague in 1538. Largely destroyed by the earthquake

Igreja do Socorro

← *Paradise on earth – apples and all kinds of fruit as far as the eye can see in Funchal's market hall*

of 1748, the present structure is richly adorned with Baroque art and carvings and now dedicated to the Mother of God. Nevertheless, there is an annual procession in honour of St James on 1 May.

Barreirinha Lido Barreirinha Lido, situated below the Igreja do Socorro, entices bathers with its pools, flume, sunbathing area, bar and restaurant.

Further north at 44, Rua Visconde Anadia, in the so-called »district between the rivers«, an **Embroidery Museum** has been installed in rooms belonging to IBTAM (Instituto de Bordados, Tapeçaria e Artesanto da Madeira), Madeira's institute for handicrafts. Beautiful examples of embroidery from the 19th century are on display, including christening robes and children's clothes from wealthy Madeiran families, as well as contemporary items (opening hours: Mon – Fri 10am – 12.30pm and 2pm – 5.30pm).

! *Baedeker* TIP

Delicate treasures

At no. 33 / 34, Rua Visconde Anadia, the biggest embroidery factory on Madeira, Patrício & Gouveia, invites visitors to take a look at the formidable amount of labour that goes into such fantastic linen and needlepoint. It quickly becomes obvious that no corners can be cut in pursuit of quality (opening hours: Mon – Fri 9am – 1pm and 3pm – 6.30pm, Sat 9.30am – noon).

The **Museum Henrique e Francisco Franco** showcases works by two brothers. Francisco Franco began his career as a sculptor in Rodin's circle in Paris and later came under criticism for his proximity to the Salazar dictatorship. His brother Henrique was a painter (opening hours: Mon – Fri 10am – 12.30pm and 2pm – 6pm).

North of Avenida Arriaga

Praça do Município To the north of the cathedral, the Praça do Município or **town hall square** is decoratively paved and graced with a fountain. It is bordered by a harmonious ensemble of Baroque houses. On the eastern side of the square stands the **town hall** (Câmara Municipal), built in 1758 as the residence of the Conde de Carvalhal, one of Madeira's richest families at the time, before it passed into the hands of the municipal administration at the end of the 19th century. The foyer is decorated with Baroque azulejos, the courtyard adorned by a sculpture, *Leda and Zeus as a Swan*. The tower served as an observation point from which to identify incoming trade ships at the earliest opportunity.

On the northwest side, the **Igreja do Colégio**, a 17th-century church of the former Jesuit College, has disappointingly irregular opening hours. Its remarkable interior is resplendent with gilded carvings and azulejos. This former college of the Jesuit order, where sons of rich Madeirans once studied, is now the seat of the University of Madeira.

Gold, silver and precious stones – such treasures are on display inside the Museu de Arte Sacra

On the southern side of the square, the Museum for Sacred Art has been housed since 1955 in what used to be the bishop's palace (17th century). The extraordinary **collection of Flemish art** from the 15th and 16th centuries shows just how valuable sugar once was. It includes pieces by Rogier van der Weyden, taken as payment for sugar shipped from Madeira. Also well worth seeing are the precious items in the cathedral treasury, including an intricately crafted, gold-plated silver Manueline processional cross (opening hours: Tue Sat 10am – 12.30pm and 2.30pm – 6pm, Sun 10am – 1pm). The Café do Museu ⊕ is a popular rendezvous for art aficionados and others.

★★
Museu de Arte Sacra

> **? DID YOU KNOW ...?**
>
> ■ The painting of St Joachim and St Anne in the Museum for Sacred Art is, in fact, said to portray King Vladislaus of Poland, better known on Madeira as Henry the German, with his wife.

The Museu do Vinho, a little to the north of the town hall square, is affiliated with the Instituto do Vinho da Madeira and houses a small yet highly informative exhibition on Madeiran viniculture (opening ⊕ hours: Mon – Fri 9am – 6pm).

Museu do Vinho

A visit to Vicentes, the photography museum at 43, Rua da Carreira, to the west of the town hall square, is an absolute treat. Vicente Gomes da Silva founded the **first photographic studio in Portugal** in

★
Museu Fotographia Vicentes

One way of decorating a wall: azulejos in the church of São Pedro

1848. His son, grandson and great grandson continued his work. As well as the original furnishings, with old optical and photographic devices, historic photos of Madeira and its inhabitants are on display, including Empress Elisabeth of Austria. The museum also houses a large photography archive (opening hours: Mon – Fri 10am – 12.30pm and 2pm – 5pm).

Church and Palace of São Pedro

The nave of the Igreja de São Pedro is decorated almost entirely with tiles from the 17th century, whilst the gilded altar is no less impressive. Opposite, inside the 18th-century Palácio de São Pedro, once the town residence of the Condes de Carvalhal, is the **Natural History Museum**. The aquarium on the ground floor presents the underwater flora and fauna of Madeira, and the upper level houses an extensive taxidermy collection reflecting Madeira's rich array of animal life (opening hours: Tue – Fri 10am – 6pm, Sat, Sun noon – 6pm).

✷ ✷ Frederico de Freitas collections

The wealthy lawyer Dr. Frederico de Freitas acquired the 17th-century residence of the Counts of Calçada in the 1940s and bequeathed it to the town on his death in 1978, complete with his extensive **arts and crafts collections**, which he had built up over many years. Faithfully maintained in the style of various epochs, the house displays furniture, paintings and everyday artefacts. The adjacent Casa dos Azulejos is home to the patron's impressive collection of tiles (opening hours: Tue – Sat 10am – 12.30pm and 2pm – 5.30pm).

The granddaughters of the island's discoverer, Zarco, probably had the Santa Clara Convent built at the end of the 15th century as a cloister for **sisters of the Order of Saint Clare**. It is situated at the top of Calçada de Santa Clara. As time progressed, the nuns came to wield considerable influence; due in no small measure to endowments, the landed estates of the convent were sizeable. The wine trade also contributed to the fortune of the Santa Clara nuns. When French corsairs invaded Funchal in 1566, pillaging the convent in the process, the nuns fled to ►Curral das Freiras. Following the death of the last sister of the Order of Saint Clare in 1890, **Franciscan nuns** took over the cloister, also establishing a nursery on the site. Today, the convent's appearance is still largely defined by the alterations and extensions undertaken in the 17th century. The Gothic portal of the convent church and the cloister with a winged altar are surviving elements of the 16th-century original construction.

✸✸
Convento de Santa Clara

The interior of the church is **completely tiled with blue, white and yellow azulejos from the 16th and 17th centuries**. The discoverer of the island, Zarco, and members of his family are buried in the chancel. Towards the rear of the nave, with its decorative, painted wood-panelled ceiling, is the Manueline-style tomb of Zarco's son-in-law, Mendes de Vasconcelos.

◄ Inside the church

Visitors are accompanied by a guide as they pass through the convent (opening hours: Mon–Fri 10am–noon and 3pm–5pm; please ring the bell).

🕒

Above the convent stands the Quinta das Cruzes. It is thought to date back to the 15th century, when it served as the residence of Zarco, the explorer who discovered the island. Destroyed to a large extent by the earthquake of 1748, it was reconstructed at the end of the 18th century. Since 1953 it has housed a **museum of cultural history**, offering insight into the lives of affluent Madeirans from the 16th to the 19th century. Items worthy of note are sugar-chest furniture, azulejos, porcelain and silver. It is worth attending one of the concerts staged here now and again just to savour the lovely atmosphere. The former residence is surrounded by a **park noted for the splendid old trees within its grounds**. Examples of stonemasonry collected from all over the island from the 15th to the 19th century are also gathered here, including Funchal's old pillory and two

✸✸
Quinta das Cruzes

A charming villa, the Quinta das Cruzes

Manueline window arches. The orchid collection in the upper section of the park is well worth seeing (opening hours: Tue – Sat 10am – 12.30pm and 2pm – 5.30pm).

Fortaleza do Pico Those who like a good walk can march up the hill to the imposing Fortaleza do Pico (17th century), now undergoing conversion to a hotel, and enjoy the magnificent panorama of Funchal and the bay (opening hours: 9am – 6pm daily).

✱ Cemitério Britânico On the west side of Rua da Carreira (no. 235), the **British Cemetery** is worth a visit. It dates back to the English occupation of Madeira (1807 – 1814); up to that time, the burial of non-Catholics and the practice of religion other than Roman Catholicism were forbidden on the island. Amongst the plots which can be found here is the family tomb of the **Blandy merchant family**, along with the grave of **William Reid**, who founded the hotel of the same name (▶Famous People; opening hours: Mon – Fri 8.30am – 5pm; regrettably, the cemetery is often closed in spite of the public opening hours).

West of the Rotunda do Infante

✱ Parque de Santa Catarina West of the Rotunda do Infante, the delightful Parque de Santa Catarina was created in the mid-20th century. It is a municipal park with flower beds, aviaries, a swan pond, a café and panoramic terrace with

Ships have changed since the era of Columbus

excellent views of the harbour. The small and simple **Capela de Santa Catarina** goes back to the 17th century. A statue of Christopher Columbus gazing into the distance stands alongside the chapel. The park features two better known **sculptures by Francisco Franco**: the bronze statue *The Sower* and – towards the harbour – a monument to the two Portuguese pilots who made the first air crossing from Lisbon to Madeira in 1921.

Beneath the Parque de Santa Catarina lies the harbour wall of the **Pontinha pier**, where cruise ships and the ferry to Porto Santo berth. Somewhat further to the west, anchored in the cargo harbour – if not out to sea – is the *Santa Maria*, a replica of Christopher Columbus' sailing vessel of the same name (▶Baedeker Tip, p. 65).

? DID YOU KNOW ...?

■ Funchal's casino is a circular concrete structure similar to the cathedral in Brasilia, also designed by Oscar Niemeyer, which evokes the crown of thorns. Born in Rio in 1907, Niemeyer is seen as a pioneer of modern architecture; his often highly unusual works are characterized by their sweeping forms.

★
Quinta Vigia

The pink-walled Quinta Vigia (formerly the Quinta das Angústias) on the west side of the Parque de Santa Catarina is now the **official residence of the regional president** and, as such, is not open to visitors. Its attractive grounds, on the other hand, which include a viewing terrace, are open to the public, even during state visits.

The original Quinta Vigia stood on the land adjacent but had to make way for the Casino and Pestana Casino Park Hotel, both designed by the Brazilian architect Oscar Niemeyer. Another resident in the Quinta Vigia of old was the Empress of Austria and Queen of Hungary, (► Famous People), who is commemorated by a bronze statue next to the hotel, looking onto Avenida do Infante.

Funchal's hotel zone is no architectural masterpiece,
but the hotels themselves are all in the superior or luxury bracket

A peaceful morning on the terrace at Reid's. Every seat is taken in the afternoon for five o'clock tea, so a reservation is strongly recommended

HOTEL WITH A HISTORY

Mere mortals approach legends with a suitable sense of awe. In this instance, a gentleman's inner sense of decorum needs to be matched by the correct attire, namely a decent shirt and tie, sharply creased trousers and shiny leather shoes. Ladies would do well to arrive in a tea-gown or cocktail dress.

Grand hotels – of which Reid's Palace Hotel is most certainly one – are equipped with a porter whose remit includes separating the wheat from the chaff at the entrance to the establishment. This is, after all, **one of the last bastions of the British Empire**.

Very British

From The Times on the breakfast table to the unshakeable institution of five o'clock tea, with scones fresh from the oven and Earl Grey served high above the Atlantic, everything is very British here. There is also a separate bridge room, of course. To spot the rather inconspicuous ent-

rance to Reid's, a certain alertness is required. The copper sign with a sweeping inscription and the narrow driveway are examples of typically British understatement, perhaps.

A dream come true

The founder of this palatial accommodation, **William Reid**, worked his way up from humble circumstances to become a highly successful wine merchant. And he was also receptive to new ideas: together with his wife Margaret, he rented out staffed quintas to wealthy visitors. Once he had acquired a sizeable piece of land, in 1887 he began work on his **grand dream** of a luxury hotel. The architect

was George Somers, previously responsible for the Shephcard Hotel in Cairo. When William Reid died a year after construction work had commenced, it was left to his sons to open the doors to the first guests.

Beautiful luxury

The hotel is impressive, to say the least: 169 rooms, **stylishly and luxuriously appointed**, the palace itself standing on a cliff top amidst over 5ha/12 acres of superb parkland with exceedingly lush tropical vegetation. Six different varieties of passion flower alone can be found here, as well as a number of tall Washingtonia palms, whilst the mighty kapok trees date back to the foundation of the hotel.

Illustrious guestbook

Many illustrious guests have come to appreciate the charm of Reid's. The guestbook naturally records visitors from the **aristocracy**, e.g. Sir Winston Churchill, Prince Edward of Great Britain or Empress Zita of Austria. World-renowned **literary figures** like Sir George Bernard Shaw and **actors** such as Gregory Peck and Roger Moore have all resided at Reid's. Not all those who check in here can lay claim to such prominence, but guests with sufficient funds at their disposal find themselves equally at home in such refined surroundings. Provided they treat the hotel's polite yet firm request with the dignified response it deserves: »evening dress to be worn from 7pm«.

Quinta Magnólia

The Quinta Magnólia is reached by following Avenida do Infante westwards and then Rua do Dr. Pita. Now owned by the government of Madeira, the building is surrounded by lush, undulating parkland. Its attractions include tennis courts and other sporting facilities, as well as a pretty playground.

! Baedeker TIP

Five o'clock tea

Everybody loves five o'clock tea at Reid's – with good reason! At around 23 € per person, it is not exactly cheap, but is an authentic British treat; to make a reservation, call 291 717 171.

South of the Quinta Magnólia, directly on the coast, stands the time-honoured **Reid's** Hotel (► Baedeker Special, p. 148). Beyond the hotel, to the right and left of the **Estrada Monumental**, which runs westwards, is the sprawl of the classic hotel zone, where the waterfront houses enjoy exclusive access to the coast. The ocean only becomes freely accessible to the public again at the popular sea-water lido. The **marine promenade** begins here and passes newer hotel complexes as far as Praia Formosa, Madeira's longest beach (800m/900yd).

Around Funchal

Jardim Botânico e Loiro Parque

Roughly 4km/2.5mi northeast of the town centre there are marvellous views from the botanical gardens. Until 1936, the estate belonged to the Reid family, the English hoteliers. Since 1952 it has been the municipal property of Funchal. Closely resembling a park, the garden has three delightful viewing points and showcases both **indigenous and imported plants**, palms, orchids, bromeliads, succulents and useful or medicinal plants. Some places within the grounds look a little neglected. The former manor house contains a small, old-fashioned museum of natural history which, in addition to a simple yet highly informative exhibition about Madeira's flora and fauna, including stuffed animals and specimens of plants, also has a collection of fossils found on the island.

Bird park ►

⏲

Colourful **parrots** from all over the world inhabit the spacious aviaries of the Loiro Parque (tropical bird park) below the botanical gardens (opening hours: 9am – 6pm daily).

Cable car ►

A cable car connects the **botanical gardens to Monte**. Covering a distance of some 1600m/5250ft, the journey takes around 14 minutes and affords splendid panoramic views across the bay of Funchal as it crosses the Ribeira de João Gomes valley with its ancient laurel woods, ending in Monte at Largo das Babosas, close to the famous pilgrimage church (► Sights from A to Z, Monte).

Jardim Orquídea

⏲

Below the bird park, on Rua Pita da Silva, the Jardim Orquídea displays all types of orchid, from seeds to blossoming plants. A mini café in the garden is a nice place to take a break and enjoy the lovely view (opening hours: 9am – 6pm daily).

Quinta do Palheiro *Map*

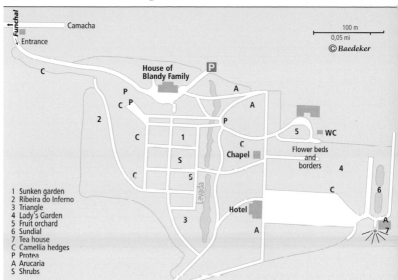

Camacha

Entrance

100 m
0,05 mi
© *Baedeker*

House of
Blandy Family

P

C

P   P

C

2

A

A

P

C

1

5   ■ WC

S

Chapel ■

Flower beds
and
borders

C

S

4

C

6

Hotel

A

A   7

1 Sunken garden
2 Ribeira do Inferno
3 Triangle
4 Lady's Garden
5 Fruit orchard
6 Sundial
7 Tea house
C Camellia hedges
P Protea
A Arucaria
S Shrubs

Approximately 10km/6mi northeast of Funchal, not far from the road to Camacha, the rambling grounds of the Quinta do Palheiro, **one of the most beautiful parks on Madeira**, are open to the public, but the admission charge is relatively steep. In 1790, the Conde de Carvalhal engaged a French landscape gardener to design the 12ha/ 30-acre estate. His first residence, now a hotel, stands in the lower part of the park. One of the count's nephews later redesigned the park in the style of an English garden – the result is a remarkably harmonious **alliance of English and French horticulture**. In 1885, the

★★
Quinta do
Palheiro
(Blandy's
Garden)

Quinta do Palheiro is one of Madeira's loveliest grand houses

Blandy family acquired the park and erected a new building in the upper half. The variety of plants in the gardens has to be seen to be believed. Many are extremely rare. The finest time to explore the gardens of the Quinta do Palheiro is when the camellias are in bloom; however, they are also famed for their lilies of the Nile, magnolias and proteas, the latter introduced by Mildred Blandy from her South African homeland. Some araucaria and decorative conifers can be seen beneath the trees. In times gone by, the frogs in the ponds were primarily destined for the count's dinner table rather than the park's atmosphere. Adjoining the grounds on the eastern perimeter is the **Palheiro Golf Club** (opening hours: Mon – Fri 9.30am – 4.30pm).

✴ Jardim do Mar

C 2 / B 2

Altitude : 0 – 175m/574ft   **Population:** approx. 1000

The idyllic alleyways of the fishing village of Jardim do Mar, the »garden of the sea«, have to be reconnoitred on foot, as the road coming to an end at a roundabout at the heart of the village.

The alleys, some paved with mosaics, all lead to the edge of the steep coast. From the roundabout, a lane leads off to the left and down to the sea, past a picturesquely situated cemetery and the ruins of a sugarcane factory to the »portinho«, or mini harbour. An **ostentatious promenade** now makes its way along the coast and a small bathing

VISITING JARDIM DO MAR

WHERE TO EAT
► Moderate
Tarmar
Sítio da Piedade
Tel. 291 823 207
On the alley leading to the small harbour basin. Simple establishment with good, somewhat overpriced, regional dishes. Attractive little terrace

WHERE TO STAY
► Budget
Hotel Jardim do Mar
Sítio da Piedade
Tel. 291 823 616, fax 291 823 617
Small, basic hotel right in the village. A few rooms have a balcony over-

looking the sea.

Baedeker recommendation

► Mid-range
Hotel Jardim Atlântico
Lombo da Rocha
Tel. 291 820 220, fax 291 820 221
www.jardimatlantico.com; 97 rooms
Far from the madding crowds, above Prazeres; sports facilities and a health and beauty »Vital Centre«. The fishing village Paúl do Mar, where it is possible to swim, is 15km/9mi away. The hotel provides a transfer service.

Paúl do Mar is one of Madeira's most unspoiled villages

area has been made. On the other side of the roundabout stands the church of Nossa Senhora do Rosário, the building of which was financed by emigrants from the village and energetically supported by the remaining inhabitants. The painted rosette is said to have been inspired by that of Notre-Dame in Paris. For the sports-minded: Jardim do Mar is **popular with surfers** on account of the powerful breakers. Large numbers of water sports enthusiasts can be seen at Ponta Jardim, one of the three pebble beaches of Jardim do Mar.

Around Jardim do Mar

Moving northeast, via a 3km/2mi long tunnel, Paúl do Mar is the next coastal settlement after Jardim do Mar. The village follows a long, narrow road along the bank and is **unique and unspoilt in character**. Two bars (one with a restaurant) offer diversion in the small fishing harbour; other localities are in the newer part of the village, further to the west, where emigrants returning from overseas reside in villas. A promenade has also been constructed here. The old centre has been upgraded with a bathing area and a large fishing sculpture. On the other hand, the small fish market hall has had to go. **Paúl do Mar**

High above Paúl do Mar, Prazeres sits on a ridge amongst fruit trees and vegetable gardens, a good **place to begin a hike through the lovely scenery** of western Madeira. Well worth seeing are the paved square in front of the church and the romantic garden of the erst- **Prazeres** while vicarage. Steep ancient connecting tracks between Jardim do Mar and Prazeres, at a height of 600m/1970ft, are used today mostly by hikers.

✳ Machico

C 7

Altitude: 0 – 150m/490ft   **Population:** approx. 12000

The fishing harbour of Machico, on the estuary of the little river bearing the same name, is Madeira's second-largest settlement, with some 12,000 inhabitants. Here, on an easily accessible stretch of coast, João Gonçalves Zarco and his followers are thought to have landed in 1419, setting foot on Madeira for the first time.

Madeira's first settlement
Not long after Zarco arrived, the first settlement was established. Under Tristão Vaz Teixeira, Machico actually became the main town in the eastern part of the island from 1440. However, when Funchal became the sole capital of Madeira in 1497, Machico's significance waned rapidly – the action shifted to the new centre on the south coast.

▶ VISITING MACHICO

INFORMATION
In the Forte Nossa Senhora do Amparo
Tel. 291 962 289

WHERE TO GO OUT
La Barca in Praçete do 25 Abril is Madeira's largest disco and even has its own parking garage for its visitors. The party starts at 11pm.

WHERE TO EAT
▶ Inexpensive
① *Amparo*
Rua da Amargura
Tel. 291 968 120
Cultivated restaurant, attached to the Residencial

② *Mercado Velho*
Rua General António Teixeira Aguiar
Tel. 291 965 926

A wonderful little spot with a terrace, beneath tall trees. Well suited for a break

WHERE TO STAY
▶ Budget
① *Hotel Dom Pedro Baía*
Estrada de São Roque
Tel. 291 969 500, fax 291 969 501
www.dompedro.com; 218 rooms
Comfortable 4-star hotel in Machico bay with a garden, swimming pool and restaurant. Ideal for families with children. Comprehensive range of sports activities on offer

② *Residencial Amparo*
Rua da Amargura
Tel. 291 968 120, fax 291 966 050
Lovely location at the heart of town behind the small fortress. Pleasant, homely rooms

Machico Map

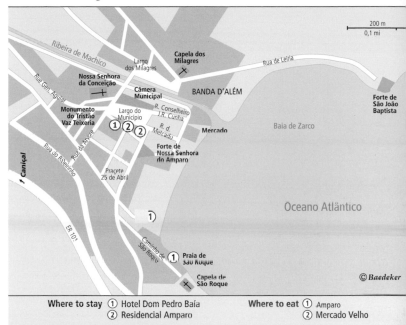

Where to stay ① Hotel Dom Pedro Baía
② Residencial Amparo

Where to eat ① Amparo
② Mercado Velho

Nevertheless, due to countless attacks by pirates between the 15th and 17th centuries, three forts were built. Today, there is a small wharf in Machico and a government school for Madeira embroidery. The place is said to be named after Robert Machyn, who according to legend was shipwrecked here with his lover Anne Dorset (►Baedeker Special, p. 34).

What to See in Machico

The real centre of Machico is the old town, situated on the west bank of the river Machico. The parish church of **Nossa Senhora da Conceição** (Our Lady of the Immaculate Conception, late 15th century) is also here. Both of the portals from the age of Manuel I are intact, as is the arch of the Vaz Teixeira mausoleum. The altars with gilded wood carvings and the painted wooden ceiling date back to the Baroque era. There is a monument commemorating Tristão Vaz Teixeira on Largo do Município. A small park alongside the pretty town hall is an inviting spot for a rest.

Old Town

The new market hall lies between the town hall and the sea. The old triangular **harbour fortress Forte Nossa Senhora do Amparo** from

Opulent gilded altar carvings proclaim the Baroque era

the 17th century stands watches over both sides of the bay. Today it houses a tourist office.

A fortress once stood beyond the promenade at the southwestern edge of the bay, since replaced by the Hotel Dom Pedro. The **Capela de São Roque** to its rear is sadly closed more often than it is open. It was erected in 1489 following a plague epidemic, with a fountain from a source believed to have miraculous properties. Some remarkable **azulejos** – scenes from the life of Saint Roch – also merit closer inspection.

On the eastern side of the harbour bay, the old **fishing district** of Banda d'Além stretches as far as the Forte São João Baptista (1800). A new promenade with a bathing area has been constructed here. Two reasons are given for the site of the **Capela dos Milagres** on Largo dos Milagres: Zarco ordained the building of a chapel here around 1420 on the tomb of Robert Machyn and Anne Dorset, some say; others claim that a Franciscan monk said mass here for the first time on Madeira on 2 July 1419. The original chapel was destroyed by floods in 1803, but the crucifix, washed away into the ocean, was discovered some days later by fishermen out at sea. This story is well illustrated in a naive painting inside the church, which was rebuilt in 1815. In honour of the figure of Christ, considered miraculous ever since, a supplicatory procession is held on 8 and 9 October.

Around Machico

Pico do Facho ✱

Northeast of Machico, the Pico do Facho (literally, peak of the torch) rises up. It earned its name by virtue of its role as a sentinel post entrusted with lighting great bonfires to forewarn the inhabitants of Machico of impending pirate attacks. On the summit of the Pico do Facho it is possible, in the right wind conditions, to witness aircraft fly past shortly after taking off from Santa Catarina Airport.

Miradouro Francisco Álvares de Nóbrega

At the southwestern entrance to the town of Machico, the Miradouro Francisco Álvares de Nóbrega, named after one of Madeira's most important poets (1773 – 1807), provides a marvellous view of the bay of Machico and the ►Ponta de São Lourenço.

★ ★ Monte

Altitude: approx. 450 – 600m/ 1450 – 1950ft

Population: 9000

In the 19th century and up to the 1940s, Monte was a popular climatic spa for wealthy Madeirans and foreigners. Numerous grand houses and villas along with some very fine hotels, graced with lush tropical gardens, testify to earlier days of tourism.

As tourists gravitated towards the coastal areas around Funchal, the status of Monte, some 8km/5mi higher up from the capital, declined. The idyllic **Largo da Fonte** (fountain square) is a reminder of former glories, with the former rack railway station and the marble chapel of Capelinha da Fonte. Just in front, leaving the main street, a steep climb up to the right leads to the restored **Quinta Jardims do Imperador**, the final residence of Karl I of Austria (►Famous People), with beautiful gardens and a tea pavilion (Caminho do Pico, Mon – Sat 9.30am – 5.30pm).

Climatic spa with tradition

⊙

The journey to Monte itself and the return leg are quite an experience in their own right, if the **cable car** (Teleférico) from Funchal is the chosen form of transport for the ascent. Looking out of the gondolas, there are splendid views of Funchal and the surrounding landscape. One way of getting back down is a basket sled (►Baedeker Tip, p. 159). From 1893, a **rack railway** ran between Monte and

★ ★
Teleférico and basket sleds

▶ VISITING MONTE

WHERE TO EAT

► Moderate

Restaurante Monte Garden
Caminho do Monte, 192
Tel. 291 780 100
The Quinta do Monte has a stylish restaurant with à-la-carte dishes. Lighter fare or just a cup of tea may be ordered in the Café Pavilion with views of Funchal.

► Inexpensive

Café do Parque
At Largo da Fonte
Basic establishment serving local dishes beneath beautiful tall trees

WHERE TO STAY

► Luxury

Quinta do Monte
Caminho do Monte, 192
Tel. 291 780 100, fax 291 780 110
www.charminghotelsmadeira.com
All 38 rooms of this marvellous quinta, close to the cable car station, have a balcony and garden view.

EVENT

Highlight of the religious festivals on Madeira is the great pilgrimage to Monte on 15 August (Assumption Day). The pilgrimage church of Nossa Senhora do Monte is resplendent with festive decorations on this day.

The pilgrimage church of Nossa Senhora do Monte houses the sarcophagus of the last Austrian Emperor, Karl I

Funchal, but after a steam boiler exploded in 1919, causing four fatalities and many serious injuries, public support for this means of conveyance cooled rapidly. The rack railway was decommissioned in 1939.

What to See in Monte

✱

Nossa Senhora do Monte

Close to the Monte cable car station, point of departure for Funchal's botanical gardens, the pilgrimage church of Nossa Senhora do Monte stands over the heart of the village. 68 steps lead up to it. Its façade, set off with dark tuff and flanked by a pair of towers, can be seen from afar. The previous church was destroyed by the earthquake of 1748 and rebuilt in Baroque style in 1818. The **view from the church terrace** across Funchal bay to Cabo Girão is marvellous.

All that is left of the original chapel is a Pietà, set in silver, in the high altar. This figure of the Virgin Mary is revered by the local population as the miraculous **patron saint of the island** and carried through the alleyways of the town in a grand procession (Romaria) every year on 15 August (Assumption Day). In the left side chapel, the plain **sarcophagus of Karl I** contains the mortal remains of the last Austrian Emperor (►Famous People).

Below the church of Monte, the Jardim Tropical Monte Palace lies in the grounds of the former Grand Hotel Belmonte – now owned by the Berardo Foundation for culture art, technology and science – and is open to visitors, although tickets are not cheap. In this imaginatively landscaped park an **abundance of art objects** can be admired, including many azulejos detailing the history of Portugal, a tiled walkway featuring works from the 15th to the 20th century, the world's largest hand-thrown vase, according to the Guinness Book of Records, over 5m/16ft tall and weighing 550kg/1210lb, an oriental garden, exhibitions of porcelain and a small mineralogical museum (opening hours 9am to 5pm daily).

★★
Jardim Tropical
Monte Palace

! **Baedeker TIP**

A sled ride at the height of summer
It may not be cheap (approx. 25 euros), but a basket sled ride from Monte down to Livramento is a must for any Madeira programme of events. Two basket sled drivers run alongside each other as they steer and brake this unique vehicle.

The entrance to the Parque ecológico do Funchal, the ecology park, can be found at the Riberia das Cales forest guard's lodge on the road from Monte to the Poiso Pass. On both sides of the well-maintained hiking trails, largely indigenous vegetation and tree species can be seen, as along a narrow **panoramic road**. This is a cul-de-sac, hence the same route back has to be followed (opening hours: 9am – 6pm daily).

Parque ecológico do Funchal

In **Terreiro da Luta**, 3km/2mi north of Monte, close to the former rack railway station a 5.5m/18ft-high statue of **Our Lady of Peace** (Nossa Senhora da Paz) stands in a marvellously scenic location. Her story goes as follows: in the First World War, a German submarine sank the French warship *Surprise* in the bay of Funchal. The Madeirans vowed to erect a monument to the Virgin Mary after the happy conclusion of the war. By 1927, enough donations had been collected to honour the promise, with the former Empress of Austria, Zita, one of the notable benefactors. A highly **unusual rosary**, crafted from the anchor chain of the sunken ship, winds its way around the plinth.

Azulejos in the Jardim Tropical

WATER IS FOR EVERYONE

One of man's greatest achievements on the island of Madeira is the elaborate irrigation system of canals, totalling some 2150km/1335mi in length. Construction of the levadas, as they are called, began around the time that the first settlers arrived on Madeira.

Madeira's first settlers were confronted with the **problem of even distribution of water**: frequent rainfall in the damp north meant that this part of the island had more than enough, whereas the much sunnier south was prone to aridity. It is not known who initiated the construction of the levadas – from the Portuguese »levar«, meaning »to lead« – but what is certain is that slaves from Africa and La Gomera, one of the Canary Islands, dug the first channels. The **island's topography** presented the most difficult obstacle, with every stone, every tool having to be carried to the most favourable route for the levada. Labourers often found themselves suspended between heaven and earth, as well as having to lower their equipment down steep rock faces by rope. Most of the levadas were actually created in the 20th century, such as the Levada dos Tornos above Funchal, through which water flowed for the first time in 1966. Measuring over 100km/60mi with approximately 100,000 outlets, it supplies water to more than 10,000 ha/24,700 acres of agricultural land.

Water and power

The levadas today still draw water from natural springs and large reservoirs which ensure that the water flows evenly. Before reaching the

A hike along the levadas reveals the beauty of the Madeiran landscape

fields, the water has already served one other useful purpose, namely as a power supply. A more efficient harnessing of this energy source can barely be conceived.

Levada law

To facilitate a fair distribution of water to farmers and peasants, levada law was established in the early years and remains largely intact today. **Levadeiros** keep the complex canal system running smoothly and oversee water distribution. Anyone who has a legitimate interest is entitled to the amount required. Landowners are thus obliged to offer up any water source within their territory for general consumption. In return, the

government does not charge for water from the levadas and pays for their upkeep.

Hiking trails

As time passes, the levadas have become more and more of a tourist attraction. The pathways alongside the canals, originally constructed for **maintenance workers**, have found favour with hikers. Not every levada trail is suitable for a hike, however. Some should only be attempted by those with a head for heights or with experience of mountainous terrain. These paths often run along rock faces with no protection from a sheer, vertical drop and are so narrow that it is just about possible to place one foot in front of the other. Fainthearted readers take note! There are also less strenuous trails, however, and whatever your level of fitness, levada hikes are a splendid way to discover Madeira's beautiful landscape.

★★ Paúl da Serra

Altitude: 1300–1400m/4225–4550ft   **Location:** 60km/38mi northwest of Funchal

The plateau of Paúl da Serra (or mountain moor), at a height of 1300–1400m/4225–4550ft, covers an area of around 102 sq km/39 sq mi and is thus Madeira's only plain of note.

Barren plateau

This **barren region, reminiscent of the Scottish Highlands** with its abundance of sheep and goats living in the wild, forms a stark contrast to the picturesque blossoms seen elsewhere in the varied landscapes of Madeira and is a paradise for hikers. The highest peak is Ruivo do Paúl (1640m/5380ft). Above a refuge maintained by the government, there is a vantage point on the Bica da Cana (1620m/5314ft) to the east.

The Paúl da Serra Plateau plays an **important role in the island's water supply**. Its porous rock behaves like an enormous sponge, soaking up precipitation. The water either flows into streams or one of the many levadas which begin their journey into the valleys here (▶Baedeker Special, p. 160). A distinctive feature of the Paúl da Serra landscape since 1993 has been the appearance of **wind turbines**.

No, this is not Scotland, but the Paúl de Serra Plateau on Madeira!

⏵ VISITING PAÚL DA SERRA

WHERE TO EAT

► Moderate
Jungle Rain Restaurant
Pico da Urze – Paúl da Serra
Tel. 291 820 150
www.hotelpicodaurze.com
From game to vegetarian dishes. This intriguingly themed restaurant adjoins a comfortable hotel.

WHERE TO STAY

► Budget
Estalagem Encumeada
Sítio dos Feiteiras – Serra de Água
Tel. 291 951 282, fax 291 951 281
Beautifully appointed small hotel with 50 rooms, some distance below the Encumeada Pass in the heart of the mountains

Encumeada Pass

The Encumeada Pass is situated at a height of 1004m/3290ft, east of the plateau at the intersection of the 110, which runs across the Paúl da Serra, and the old mountain road, the 228, which was the only connection by road between São Vicente on the north coast and Ribeira Brava on the south coast before the tunnels were completed. On a clear day, the vantage point presents excellent **views of the mountainous landscape** and **the ocean beyond the north and south coasts**.

✷ ✷
Vantage point

Rabaçal

Rabaçal (1064m/3490ft) lies in a striking valley cutting at the western end of the Paúl da Serra and basically consists of a few deserted inns. The surrounds are truly breathtaking, richly forested with ancient laurel and tree heath, interspersed with a wide variety of ferns, moss and lichen. The area around Rabaçal is a very **popular destination for weekenders** who can enjoy any of a number of delightful picnic areas. The name of the place means something like »untouched«. An old lane which leads down to Rabaçal has been closed to traffic, so hikers have to leave their vehicles in the unsecured car park on the plateau. Nevertheless, the descent into the valley is well worth the effort!

! *Baedeker* TIP

Guided hiking tours

There are no public transport services to Rabaçal. Those wishing to explore the valley should start out early – whether by taxi or with a hire car. Alternatively, almost all local tour operators run trips to Rabaçal.

A challenging hike, best left well alone by vertigo sufferers, is the trail from Rabaçal to the **»25 Fontes«** (»25 springs«), taking around 2 hours. Here a number of gushing streams flow in small cataracts into

The most popular walks

Suitable for children – a walk near Rabaçal

a mere which, depending on the time of year, may or may not be full. The water of this decidedly picturesque little lake feeds the Levada do Risco. An easier hike, half an hour in duration, follows this particular levada to the **Risco waterfalls**, which boast some of Madeira's most spectacular cataracts in the wetter months of the year. The path for both hikes commences at the former car park in Rabaçal. After some 200m/200yd natural steps lead down to the »25 springs« to the right. To reach the waterfalls, continue straight ahead rather than following the steps.

★ ★ Pico Ruivo · Pico do Arieiro

B/C 5

Madeira's highest peak

North of Funchal, at the centre of the island, are Madeira's highest mountains, the Pico Ruivo (1862m/6100ft), the Pico das Torres (1851m/6070ft) and the Pico do Arieiro (1818m/5960ft). In the late morning, cloud cover often impairs the view, so it is advisable to set off early in the day.

Above the clouds

Pico Ruivo is Madeira's highest mountain. Even when the lower reaches of the island are shrouded in thick mist, its rugged, ruddy peaks can often still be seen in clear sunshine – the hike to the top reveals how varied the Madeiran weather can be.

Pico do Arieiro is the third-highest mountain on the island – and at the same time **the most easily accessible**. A decent road ends just a few metres below the summit, bringing Funchal within an hour's reach. The final, 7km/4mi stretch of road, branching off at Paso de Poiso, initially passes through dense woodland which gives way to increasingly open heathland before arriving in rocky, cragged mountain terrain with breathtaking views. A number of vantage points along this road provide magnificent views of Madeira, provided the weather remains fair. There is a small bar on the plateau at the summit. A simple path leads down from the pousada to the **Miradouro do Juncal** viewpoint (1800m/5905ft), where there is a panorama of Madeira's northern coast.

The hike from Pico do Arieiro to Pico Ruivo takes around four hours and is extremely worthwhile, but requires **stamina and sound equipment**. The magnificent panorama of the entire island from the summit is more than ample reward for such efforts (▶ Practicalities: Hiking).

✳ ✳
From Pico do Arieiro to Pico Ruivo

A break with stupendous views at the Pico do Arieiro

✳ Ponta Delgada

B 5

Altitude: approx. 10 – 165m/32 – 541ft   **Population:** approx. 2500

The small town of Ponta Delgada on the north coast of Madeira boasts a popular seawater swimming pool. Powerful breakers constantly replenish the basin with fresh water from the ocean.

Picturesque pilgrimage site
Fruit and vegetable cultivation are of economic significance here, whilst much of the osier used in Madeiran basketry also grows here. In and around Ponta Delgada there is a noticeably large number of quintas, built by the grand winegrowers who accumulated their riches in the 18th century. Down by the sea is the old heart of the town, with the new town higher up on the other side of the through road.

What to See in and Around Ponta Delgada

✳ Capela do Bom Jesus
Every year in Ponta Delgada, on the first Sunday in September, **one of the oldest religious festivals** on Madeira takes place. The occasion relates to a legend from the year 1470, when a chest containing

The newly restored sea front of Ponta Delgada

a wooden crucifix was washed up on the shore – just as a small chapel was about to be built there, thus earning it the name of Capela do Bom Jesus. In 1908 the pilgrimage church completely burned down. Nothing survived, save for the charred remnants of the cross, preserved since then in a glass case inside the new church (1919) and revered by the religious local population. The **unusual fresco adorning the church ceiling** is striking: it includes depictions of paradise and a ship of the Knights of Christ, symbolizing the Portuguese discoveries. The beautifully located rest home close to the church was originally a pilgrim hostel.

Southeast of Ponta Delgada, the coastal road leaves the ocean and after 2km/just over a mile reaches **Boaventura** (3000 inhabitants), nestled between fruit

⊙ VISITING PONTA DELGADA

WHERE TO EAT

► Moderate

Solar de Boaventura
Tel. 291 860 888
www.solar-boaventura.com
Neat restaurant in Boaventura,
sometimes serving game. The Solar de
Boaventura is also a good place to
spend the night.

WHERE TO STAY

► Mid-range

Monte Mar Palace Hotel
Ponta Delgada

Tel. 291 860 030, fax 291 860 031
www.montemar-palace.com; 105
rooms
Modern, pleasantly appointed 4-star
hotel. Anyone desiring comfortable
accommodation on the north coast
need look no further.

► Budget

Corte do Norte
Ponta Delgada
Tel. 291 862 070
Fax 291 862 072; 11 rooms
Small, basic hotel and restaurant

---

gardens and sprawling **osier plantations for local basket weaving**.
The basis of this region's fertility is the plentiful water supply, as a
number of small rivers originating in the central mountains flow
through here on their way to the Atlantic. Boaventura itself has little
in the way of sights, but is ideal for relaxing in lovely surroundings.
Many visitors to the island see Boaventura as an ideal starting point
for attractive hikes.

✹✹ Ponta de São Lourenço

C 8/9

Altitude: 0 322m/1056ft   **Location:** 34km/21mi east of Funchal

**Raw cliffs, coarse vegetation and a predominantly stiff, head-on
breeze – this is the east of Madeira, a fascinating contrast to the
lush greenery which thrives elsewhere on the island.**

Ponta de São Lourenço has more in common with Porto Santo than
Madeira in terms of sparse vegetation. It can be reached via a road
tunnel, 750m/800yd in length, at ► Caniçal. The road ends at a car
park, high above Abra Bay, with a view into the distance over a **near-
vertical drop and rugged rock formations** along the coast. To the
northeast, the neighbouring island of ► Porto Santo can be seen, to
the southeast the Ilhas Desertas. The stratification of some of the
cliffs of Ponta de São Lourenço provides a compelling insight into
the volcanic origins of the island. Numerous wind turbines generate
energy for the industrial and free trade zone of Caniçal.

*Madeira's
eastern
peninsula*

The fissured eastern peninsula of Madeira, the Ponta de São Lourenço, offers clues to the island's volcanic origins ...

Accessible only on foot Starting at the car park, a **rewarding hike** (around 4 hours there and back) follows dirt tracks as they make their way through impressive terrain, a nature reserve, to Ponta do Furado, the easternmost tip of the peninsula; in misty conditions, however, it is safer not to set out. Surefootedness and solid footwear are essential.

Ilhéu do Farol, Ilhéu de Agostinho Off the coast of Ponta do Furado lie the deserted islands of Ilhéu de Agostinho and Ilhéu do Farol, the latter with a lighthouse erected in 1870 which marks the **easternmost point of Madeira**.

Ponta do Pargo

B 1

Altitude: 473m/1550ft   **Population:** approx. 1100

The sleepy village of Ponta do Pargo is Madeira's westernmost settlement and scene of an annual apple festival in September. All imaginable manifestations of the fruit are celebrated. The land here is so flat that tractors can be deployed on the fields – practically the only region of Madeira where this is the case!

... whilst the western tip of the island, with Portugal's highest lighthouse, resembles the bow of a ship

20km/13mi of sinuous road connect Calheta and Ponta do Pargo, **Westernmost** the journey taking roughly one hour. Those undaunted by the trip **point of Madeira** will find themselves rewarded by two quaint attractions: a short road leads to **Portugal's highest lighthouse** (392m/1286ft), crowned in bright red paint. It is situated around 1.5km/1mi outside the village at the westernmost point of Madeira, signalling to ships the safest route around the island and presenting fine views of the west. Inside the lighthouse is a small, interesting exhibition on Portuguese lighthouses (opening hours: 9.30am – noon and 2pm – 4.30pm daily). Equally worthwhile is the view from the **Miradouro**, at a distance of around 1km/0.5mi.

PONTA DO PARGO

WHERE TO EAT

▶ **Inexpensive**

O Farol

On the road leading to the lighthouse
Tel. 291 880 010
A friendly restaurant, belonging to a small, modern hotel

In the late 1990s, the small church of Ponta do Pargo, dedicated to Saint Peter, was enhanced with an unusually **colourful ceiling fresco** featuring paradisiacal landscapes.

✷ Ponta do Sol

C 3

Altitude: approx. 30 – 180m/100 – 590ft

Population: approx. 4500

Ponta do Sol was home to the grandfather of the US author John Roderigo dos Passos (1896 – 1970), who found international fame with *The 42nd Parallel* and *Manhattan Transfer*.

Bananas, poets and tourists

Ponta do Sol, on the south coast of Madeira, was founded as early as 1450, granted its town charter in 1501 and was, for many years, a centre of sugarcane cultivation. Today, sugarcane has given way to **banana plantations**. Produce from one of Madeira`s biggest banana packing plants is transported from the town, its by lorry to Funchal before leaving the country on export.

The grandfather of **John dos Passos** emigrated to the USA in the 19th century. His grandson visited his ancestor's homeland on a number of occasions, the last visit being in 1960. A commemorative plaque can be seen on the former family home in Rua Príncipe D. Luís I, more recently converted into a **cultural centre**.

Ponta do Sol's ambitions of becoming a more lively tourist destination have only been partially realized, although the place is a popular port of call for almost every organized tour of the island. In addition to its picturesque seafront promenade, it offers a restful and relaxed environment.

Afternoon sun over Ponta do Sol, with the church of Nossa Senhora da Luz

◉ VISITING PONTA DO SOL

WHERE TO EAT

► **Moderate**

Poente
Cais da Ponta do Sol
Tel. 291 973 579
Renowned for its fish and located
above the beach at Ponta do Sol

WHERE TO STAY

► **Budget**

Baía do Sol
Rua Dr. João Augusto Teixeira
Tel. 291 970 140

Fax 291 970 149
www.enotel.com; 71 rooms
The hotel is situated on the short
promenade of Ponta do Sol, neatly
concealed behind old façades. Comfortably appointed, modern design

SHOPPING

A wide selection of Madeiran and
Portuguese wines can be purchased at
Adega da Vila in Ponta Sol Shopping,
Estrada do 5 Centenário

What to See in Ponta do Sol

Arriving from Ribeira Brava, the finest view of this picturesque little
town, flanked by high rock faces, can be enjoyed from above the
»Point of the Sun« on the road which meanders its way into the valley. The inviting alleyways and steps between the houses, bedecked
with flowers, are perfect for a leisurely stroll.

Picturesque townscape

The church of Nossa Senhora da Luz (Our Lady of the Light) stands
on the site of an earlier structure from the 15th century. Tangible
relics from the original church are confined to a statue of the patron
saint and a baptismal font said to have been donated by King Manuel
I himself. The present church was renovated in colourful, intricate
Baroque style, with the **original wooden Mudéjar ceiling** retained
in the chancel, albeit repainted in the style of the day.

★
Nossa Senhora da Luz

Just 2km/about a mile higher up, in the district of Lombada, the
Quinta de João Esmeraldo stands at the heart of extensive banana
plantations. In the 15th century its landlord, a **companion of Christopher Columbus**, ran one of Madeira's largest sugarcane plantations with hundreds of slaves. The
pink mansion, also said to have been frequented by Columbus, now
belongs to the regional government and serves as a school. Opposite,
the Espírito Santo chapel features beautiful wood carvings and
azulejos.

! *Baedeker* **TIP**

Levada tour
A short, steep wooden ladder and a snaking path
connect the two levadas in the valley of Ponta do
Sol, so it is possible to make a round trip on foot.

★★ Porto Moniz

A 2 / 3

Altitude: approx. 10 – 280m/30 – 900ft **Population:** approx. 3500

The coastal road winds its way from the west in countless twists and turns down to the ocean and Porto Moniz, at the northwesternmost point of the island.

Popular summer resort The little town has long been a popular summer resort for tourists and Madeirans alike; its infrastructure has developed considerably and the new coastal promenade bears witness to a modernization programme.

Wine growing complements tourism as an important economic factor. The town's name honours the Portuguese nobleman Francisco Moniz, who settled here in 1533. Thanks to an outcrop of rock that juts far out into the ocean and the Ilhéu Mole, complete with lighthouse, Porto Moniz is the best-protected harbour on Madeira's northern coast and was a whaling station for many years.

● VISITING PORTO MONIZ

INFORMATION
Vila do Porto Moniz
Tel. 291 852 555

WHERE TO EAT
► **Moderate**
Salgueiro
Lugar do Tenenente
Tel. 291 852 139
Decent Madeiran cuisine, fish in particular. Narrow terrace in the direction of the swimming pool

► **Inexpensive**
Pérola do Norte
Vila do Porto Moniz
Tel. 291 853 000
Pleasant, friendly restaurant. The grilled fish is especially good.

WHERE TO STAY
► **Budget**
Residencial Calhau
Sítio das Poças
Tel. 291 853 104
Fax 291 853 443
Simple, tastefully appointed guest-house above the seawater swimming pool

Euro Moniz
Vila do Porto Moniz
Tel. 291 850 050
Fax 291 853 933
www.euromoniz.com; 33 rooms
Agreeable little hotel in the town, with swimming pool and restaurant. Panoramic bar on the top floor

MARKET
The Feira de Porto Moniz, a large agricultural fair with stalls, espetada kiosks and a cattle market is usually held over a July weekend.

Fun in the Piscinas Naturais at Porto Moniz

What to See in Porto Moniz

Amongst the most popular attractions are the **natural swimming pools of lava rock** which have formed along the deeply fissured coast. The surf ensures that the water is constantly renewed, as waves wash over into the basin. There is a small entrance fee for the **Piscinas Naturais** seawater pools, but changing rooms, lounging areas and a snack bar are on hand.

★★
Lava swimming pools

The new centre for life sciences is situated on the coastal promenade, featuring temporary exhibitions — fascinating for children too (opening hours Tue – Sun 10am – 7pm).

Centro de Ciência Viva
🕐

Parts of the old São João Baptista fort, which protected the settlement from pirates in days gone by, have been reconstructed at the harbour and a small **aquarium** (opening hours: 10am – 6pm daily) established. A helipad has also been built, along with ample mooring berths for yachts.

Harbour
🕐

Around Porto Moniz

The road beyond Porto Moniz follows the north coast. The new road progresses through unspectacular tunnels for long stretches, whilst the older road is now a one-way, single-lane affair running east to west. Leaving Porto Moniz, Seixal is reached in no time at all. The return journey is quite an adventure: the roadway is cut into the rock

★★
Round trip on the north coast

face, a route leading through narrow tunnels and beneath waterfalls – convertibles should keep the hood up to save the occupants from getting wet.

✳
Ribeira da Janela

Ribeira da Janela lies southeast of Porto Moniz on the river of the same name, which leaves its deep valley bed here as it flows into the sea. Three rock formations rise up from the water, one of which, the Ilhéu da Ribeira da Janela, gave the place and the river their names on account of a **naturally occurring opening, shaped like a window** (in Portuguese: »janela« = window). The village itself, higher up the valley at a height of 450m/1475ft, is well worth a visit. Its lofty location and attractive townscape are matched by **marvellous scenery** in the surrounding area. A little-used road winds its way up to the Paúl da Serra plateau. Ribeira da Janela played an important role in the construction of **hydroelectric power stations** in a programme initiated during the Salazar dictatorship in the 1970s. Today, Madeira has four such hydropower stations, although they account for only a relatively modest share of the island's electricity. Part of the island's energy supply is now generated by wind turbines.

✳✳ Porto Santo

Inset map

Altitude: 0 – 517m/1696ft

Location: 43km/26mi northeast of the main island of Madeira

Porto Santo is also known as the »golden island«. The lush vegetation which makes Madeira so attractive is absent here, but Porto Santo does have something in abundance which is virtually nonexistent on Madeira: turquoise-coloured water and a splendid, golden-yellow sandy beach, some 9km/5.5mi in length and said to be healthy, although there is no real scientific evidence to support the claim.

Five small, rocky islands surround the island of Porto Santo, which lies 43km/27mi northeast of Madeira. Roughly 11km/6.5mi long and approx. 6km/3.5mi wide, Porto Santo has an area of 42.5 sq km/17 sq mi, its highest point being Pico do Facho at 517m/1703ft. The **mineral springs** on this otherwise predominantly dry island are said to be effective against rheumatism, calcium deficiency and other ailments. Earlier, limestone was mined on Ilhéu de Baixo off the coast to the south, then fired on Porto Santo and sold as fertilizer or mortar to Madeira. Porto Santo currently has around 5000 inhabitants, who earn their living from **fishing and making wine** or, increasingly in more recent times, from **tourism**. There is also an airport, constructed by NATO in 1960.

▶ VISITING PORTO SANTO

GETTING THERE

A daily ferry sails between Madeira and Porto Santo (a two-hour trip). A faster way of completing the journey is by turboprop aircraft, with several flights a day taking off from Santa Catarina Airport (approx. 20 mins).

INFORMATION

Av. Henrique Vieira e Castro
Tel. 291 985 189

SPORT

Swimming is just one of the many sports suited to Porto Santo. The energetic can try their hand at sailing, surfing, riding or cycling.

WHERE TO EAT

▶ Moderate
Salinas
Rua Goulart Medeiros
Vila Baleira
Good international fare right on the beach, on the edge of town

▶ Inexpensive
Marques
Rua João Santana, 9
Vila Balcira
Tel. 291 982 319
Simple, tasty dishes with a local flavour

WHERE TO STAY

▶ Mid-range
Hotel Torre Praia
Rua Goulart Medeiros
Vila Baleira
Tel. 291 980 450, fax 291 982 487
www.torrepraia.pt
Modern hotel at the beach in Vila Baleira, with swimming pool and sun terrace

Hotel Apartamentos Luamar
Cabeço da Ponta
Tel. 291 984 121, fax 291 983 100
Well-groomed, mid-range hotel with 71 rooms, situated on the most attractive stretch of beach, west of Vila Baleira. Comfortable rooms, swimming pool and comprehensive sporting facilities

▶ Budget
Pensão Central
Rua C. A. Magno Vasconcelos, 1
Tel. 291 982 226
Fax 291 983 460; 42 rooms
Hotel with basic rooms in Vila Baleira, a little way from the beach

The beautiful sandy beach on the south coast and good infrastructure have led to a constant increase in tourism in recent years. During the summer holidays, Porto Santo is particularly popular with Madeiran families. The even climate means it is possible to swim in the sea at any time of year. There is a thalassotherapy centre in Cabeço, south of the main city. The newest attraction is a golf course in the south, between Capela de São Pedro and the north coast.

★ ★
Homely holiday island

Sand, sand and more sand, some 9km/5.5mi of beach …

Reforestation   Porto Santo was once densely covered with dracaena, junipers and heather. The first settlers cleared the fertile land to cultivate grain, earmarked for Portuguese expeditions overseas, a lucrative business. However, the land soon karstified and the earth was washed away by rainwater. Grain cultivation revived in the 18th century, as evidenced by windmills in the landscape. Today, there is relatively little in the way of cultivation of grain, grapes, fruit or vegetables, but efforts are being made to return the terrain to its verdant state through intensive reforestation.

History   João Gonçalves Zarco and Tristão Vaz Teixeira sought out the archipelago in 1418 and first explored the more easily accessible Porto Santo (»Holy Harbour«). In 1419, they returned with Bartolomeu Perestrelo, who set about cultivating the land with the aid of Portuguese settlers. Porto Santo's most celebrated inhabitant was Christopher Columbus (►Famous People), who is thought to have spent a number of years on the island around 1450 with his wife Filipa Moniz, Perestrelo's daughter. In the 16th and 17th centuries pirate raids became such a concern that the islanders erected fortifications and, on occasion, seriously considered moving across to Madeira.

Christopher Columbus ►

Porto Santo Map

Oceano

Ilhéu de Fora

Baixa dos Barbeiros

Baixa do Meio

Atlântico

Ilhéu da Fonte da Areia

Ilhéu das Cenouras

Camacha

Serra de Dentro

Fonte da Areia

▲ Pico do Facho

▲ Pico do Castelo

✈

Dragoal

Serre del Fora

Tanque

Porto Abrigo

Vila Baleira

Ilhéu de Ferro

Campo de Cima

© *Baedeker*

Campo de Baixo

▲ Pico de Ana Ferreira

Ilhéu de Cima

○ Ponta

5 km
3 mi
© *Baedeker*

Ilhéu de Baixo ou da Cal

What to See on Porto Santo

The **main settlement and harbour**, Vila Baleira, formerly Porto San-to, is situated on the flat south coast of the island. This modest town has an unhurried air, in spite of being home to the majority of Porto Santo's population. It contains a market hall, a handful of small hotels, guesthouses and restaurants. The new market hall stands almost on the seafront, whilst a craft centre (Centro de Artesania) featuring various shops is located on Rua Manuel Gregório Pestana jun. The main square of Vila Baleira is the beautifully paved **Largo do Pelourinho**, meeting point for locals and tourists. »Pelourinho« means

Vila Baleira

pillory, and one stands in the square as a symbol of jurisdiction. The plain white parish church of **Nossa Senhora da Piedade** was rebuilt after it was pillaged by pirates in 1667. Its most attractive feature is the azulejo of a Pietà which graces the outer wall. The **town hall** (Câmara Municipal), a fine architectural example of Portuguese Renaissance architecture, also stands on Largo do Pelourinho.

An appealing little museum in the **Casa Museu Cristóvão Colombo**, where Columbus is purported to have lived, displays all manner of artefacts from daily life, marine charts, documents and depictions of the history of seafaring and the like (opening hours Tue – Sat 10am – 12.30pm, 2pm – 5.30pm, Sun 10am – 1pm, July – Sept until 7pm).

Other Places on Porto Santo

Nossa Senhora da Graça   On the road from Vila Baleira heading northeast, the small church of Nossa Senhora da Graça was constructed in 1951 on the site of a

Once the residence of Christopher Columbus, now the Columbus Museum

chapel dating back to the 15th century. It is venerated on account of a miraculous mineral spring. The island's most important religious festival is held here annually on 15 August (Feast of the Assumption).

From the Portela viewpoint further to the east, fine views across the south and east of Porto Santo, with the small island of Ilhéu de Cima and its lighthouse, can be enjoyed. **Portela viewpoint**

North of Porto Santo rises the tree-covered Pico do Castelo (437m/ 1433ft), an extinct volcano, cone-like in shape. At the summit, the scant remains of a 16th-century fortress still stand. There is a monument to the instigator of the reforestation efforts. In Camacha, north of the Pico do Castelo **traditional wine is produced** – these days with up-to-date methods. The wine can be sampled here. Beyond Camacha on the north coast, the waters of the **Fonte da Areia** are said to help alleviate stomach, bowel and skin ailments. Some consider it to be a veritable fountain of youth. Those who are simply hungry or thirsty can stop off for a picnic. **Pico do Castelo**

! *Baedeker* TIP

Taking it easy or ready for some sport?
Porto Santo's coastal cycle path stretches for 10km/ 6mi along even terrain, parallel to golden sandy beaches. A full circuit of the island demands considerably greater exertions – thanks to three serious climbs.

Pico de Ana Ferreira (283m/928ft) in the western part of the island features interesting **formations of basalt columns**. The simple Capela de São Pedro (17th/18th century), which only opens its doors to the public on St Peter's Day (29 June), is perched on its southern face. Golfers will be pleased to find an 18-hole course close by, with another golf course in the planning stages. **Pico de Ana Ferreira**

From Ponta da Calheta, a popular swimming spot at the **southwestern tip of Porto Santo**, there are marvellous views of Ilhéu de Baixo off the coast and, on a clear day, Madeira and the Ilhas Desertas. Restaurants in the vicinity serve exquisite fish dishes. There have been discussions concerning the installation of a cable car connection between the main island and the Ilhéu de Baixo, but a wave of protest from conservationists, fearing the worst for the bird colonies which breed there, has led to an inquiry into the environmental sustainability of the project before any decision is taken. **Ponta da Calheta**

The only campsite on the entire Madeira archipelago, the Parque do Campismo on Rua Goulart Medeiros in Vila Baleira, Porto Santo, tel. 291 982 160, fax 291 982 584, is open throughout the year. Further details on the website at www.madeira-camping.com. **Madeira's only campsite**

✳ Ribeira Brava

C / D 4

Altitude: approx. 30 – 180m/98 – 590ft   **Population:** approx. 9000

Ribeira Brava came to prominence as the point at which the north-south axis across the Encumeada Pass and an east-west trading route intersected. Merchants and traders met in Ribeira Brava to conduct their business.

»Wild river« Ribeira Brava, an erstwhile fishing village at the mouth of the wild watercourse of the same name, lies on Madeira's southwest coast. In the summer months little more than a glorified rill, winter rainfall can see it swell rapidly to a raging torrent – hence the name **»wild river«**. As the communications infrastructure improved, the village enjoyed a certain degree of prosperity, developing into a favoured weekend destination amongst the local population. As a consequence, numerous apartment houses have sprung up behind the old centre. These can be bypassed by tunnel, whilst a wide, attractive promenade with sweeping open spaces has been constructed on the seafront. A further attraction is the black beach with a seawater swimming pool and gigantic fountain.

What to See in Ribeira Brava

Spruce townscape A half-hour walk suffices to see a number of handsome examples of typical Madeiran architecture: colourful window shutters, wrought-iron balcony railings and fine façades. The remains of an old fort, constructed in the 17th century to guard against corsair raids, can be seen on the river promenade. Today, the tourist information office is located here.

 VISITING RIBEIRA BRAVA

INFORMATION
In Forte de São Bento
Tel. 291 951 675

WHERE TO EAT
▶ **Moderate**
Restaurante Água Mar
Estrada Regional/
Rua Engenheiro Ribeiro Pereira
Tel. 291 951 148
Freshly caught fish and crustaceans
are house specialities.

WHERE TO STAY
▶ **Budget**
Hotel Bravamar
Rua Comandante Camacho Freitas
Tel. 291 952 224
Fax 291 951 122; 70 rooms
A comfortable house with restaurant
and bar, not far from the riverside
road

On an ornately paved square in the centre stands the Igreja de São Bento, a pretty village church from the 16th century, its **tower covered with blue and white tiles** and crowned with an armillary sphere. The font is thought to have been donated by King Manuel I in 1500. Also worthy of inspection are a Manueline pulpit, splendid Baroque altars and a number of elaborate azulejos. Valuable Flemish paintings can be seen on the sides of the chancel.

Just a few steps from the church, Ribeira Brava's town hall, a well-preserved **mansion** built in 1776, stands amidst beautiful, park-like gardens, ideal for a break.

Those interested in the **history of Madeira** should pay a visit to the **modern museum of ethnography** (Museo Etnográfico). The layout is both interesting and entertaining, offering an insight into Madeiran fishing, the Madeiran countryside, viniculture and cooperage, as well as much worth knowing about the weaving trade; old basket sleds and ox-

The church of Ribeira Brava and festive decorations

carts are also on display. Appealing craftwork is sold in the museum shop (opening hours: Tue – Sun 10am – 12.30pm and 2pm – 6pm).

★ Ribeiro Frio

C 6

Altitude: 860m/2821ft   **Population:** approx. 100

At the heart of a mountain landscape and the last uninterrupted area of laurisilva forest on the island, the small settlement of Ribeiro Frio – »cold river« in translation – tends to be rather busy at times. All the bus tours on the island converge here to visit the trout farms which have been set up on the initiative of the state.

A comfortable seat, a drink and tasty trout in Victor's Bar ...

What to See in Ribeiro Frio

✳ **Trout farming**
Trout are bred in basins arranged in terraces and supplied with oxygen-rich water from the Ribeiro Frio river. The fish are sold to caterers and restaurants or cast into the wild streams of the island for anglers to catch. The trout farming station at Ribeiro Frio is a pleasure for all the senses: the basins are integrated into a quaint little park with fragrant box hedges.

▶ RIBEIRO FRIO

WHERE TO EAT
▶ **Inexpensive**
Victor's Bar
Tel. 291 575 898
Rustic restaurant for trippers, serving – surprise, surprise – delicious fresh trout (Portuguese: truta)

Behind Victor's Bar lies the Parque Florestal, a nature reserve and **UNESCO World Heritage site**, intended to protect the primordial **laurisilva forest** which has survived on the island. Many endemic species of plants growing here are also to be safeguarded against extinction.

✳ **A hike to the Balcões viewing point**
From Ribeiro Frio, a hiking trail which follows the Levada do Furado comes complete with the considerable reward of the viewing point at Balcões. The simple hike lasts for something like one hour (there and back) and passes through splendid scenery on its way to the viewing point, with **marvellous views of the highest peaks on Madeira** – Pico Ruivo, Pico das Torres and Pico do Arieiro. Those who feel fit enough, have a head for heights and are steady on their feet can walk in the opposite direction along the Levada do Furado as far as Portela.

✳ Santa Cruz

C 7

Altitude: 0 – 150m/490ft   **Population:** approx. 10,000

The fishing town of Santa Cruz on the south coast of Madeira has remained largely unchanged over the years. Due to its proximity to Santa Catarina Airport, this delightful place is barely on the tourist radar.

A beautifully paved waterfront promenade, lined with palm trees, is an inviting setting for a stroll. The pebble beach, with its colourful fishing boats and shady palm trees, is also as pretty as a picture. At the edge of town, the popular **Praia das Palmeiras swimming complex** attracts bathers.

Waterfront stroll

What to See in Santa Cruz

The quaint and narrow alleyways of the old town lend it a strikingly homogeneous appearance. The 16th-century town hall, embellished with Manueline stonemasonry, is worthy of note. Close to the church, the courthouse with its curved flight of steps also merits a look.

✳ **Homogeneous ensemble**

Having grown rich on the profits of sugarcane cultivation, the community built itself **Madeira's second-largest church after the Sé in Funchal**. The parish church of São Salvador was constructed in 1533 on the remains of an older chapel. A tomb dating back to 1470 is a survivor of the original building. The sacristy contains 16th-century azulejos that once graced the walls of Nossa Senhora da Piedade, the Franciscan monastery that gave way to the airport. Evidence of Manueline style can be found in a window and a portal in the choir.

> **!** *Baedeker* TIP
>
> ### Fun on the slide!
>
> The new water park in Santa Cruz is a winner with families in particular: two swimming pools (one for children) with the »Lazy River« flowing around them, five toboggan runs and four fast slides — fun is guaranteed.

 VISITING SANTA CRUZ

WHERE TO EAT
► **Inexpensive**
Praia das Palmeiras
In the swimming complex
Tasty fish dishes on the terrace await those who have worked up a hunger in the water.

WHERE TO STAY
► **Mid-range**
Hotel Santa Catarina
Rua do Bom Jesus
Tel. 291 520 000, fax 291 520 001
Modern hotel with 40 rooms, attractive garden, gaming room and the Restaurant Loural

The pebble beach of Santa Cruz is a peaceful idyll

Market hall Situated right on the seafront, the Santa Cruz market hall is especially inviting. A rich variety of fish is on offer, as well as fruit and vegetables from the region. Modern azulejos decorate the building.

✳ Santana

`B 6`

Altitude: 420m/1377ft   **Population:** approx. 4500

At the heart of Madeira's most fertile region lies Santana. Surrounded by floral splendour, Santana's beautiful thatched houses underline the town's status as one of the most picturesque spots on the island.

What to See in and Around Santana

✳ Casas de Colmo The traditional Casas de Colmo (straw houses) are **listed buildings, their triangular straw roofs extending down to the ground** to protect the interior from the ravages of the weather. Today, there are far fewer of these houses than in the past on account of their elaborate roofs, which are expensive to maintain and have to be renewed regularly. The local council has erected two such houses alongside the town hall – one of which serves as the tourist information office.

Madeira yesterday, today and tomorrow An interesting place to visit in Santana is the **theme park for the history and culture of Madeira** (Parque Temático da Madeira). Four pavilions focus on, among other things, the island's discovery and the future of the entire planet. Extreme sports such as bungee jumping and climbing are also on offer. The 7 ha/17-acre site also boasts a replica of the historic Monte rack railway train and a small lake with

► VISITING SANTANA

INFORMATION
Sítio do Serrado
Tel. 291 572 992

MARKET
Farmer's market with flowers, vegetables, fruit and honey, every Sunday from 10am on the road to Pico Ruivo

WHERE TO STAY
► Budget
O Colmo
Santana Sítio do Serrado
Tel. 291 570 290
Fax 291 574 312, 40 rooms
Most pleasant hotel in the centre of Santana with indoor swimming pool and sauna

Residencial O Cortado
Tel. 291 572 240
Fax 291 573 538
Two houses on the fairly noisy road between Faial and Santana. Ocean views from the higher of the two, the lower is more simply appointed.

It is also possible to sleep under a straw roof in one of two Casas de Colmo.

WHERE TO EAT
► Inexpensive
Restaurante O Pescador
Sítio Pico António Fernandes
Tel. 291 572 272
Excellent cuisine in an elegant atmosphere. Superb fish and a variety of delicious lamb dishes

Baedeker recommendation

► Moderate
Quinta do Furão
Achada do Gramacho
Tel. 291 570 100
www.quintadofurao.com
North of Santana, on the coast with great sea views. Excellent cuisine in quite distinctive surroundings. A modern hotel also on site

miniature fishing boats. Two restaurants and a bar keep hunger at bay (opening hours 10am – 7pm daily, closed on 25 December). ⏰

From the outskirts of Santa, a cable car (Teleférico) leads down the steep coastline to Rocha do Navio (Sat, Sun, Wed; exact timetable available from the tourist information office in Santana). The beach below is not particularly inviting, but the journey reveals spectacular scenery.

Cable car to Rocha do Navio

A pleasant excursion from Santana leads to the Casa das Queimadas (883m/2896ft), a forest ranger lodge with picnic areas in the mountains southwest of Santana. Continuing south, hikers arrive at the lush **Parque Florestal das Queimadas** on the slopes of Pico Ruivo (1862m/6108ft), whose summit can be reached from here.

★
Excursion to the Casa das Queimadas

✳ Santo da Serra

C 7

Altitude: 675m/2214ft   **Population:** approx. 2000

Santo da Serra – Santo António da Serra, to give it its full name – is situated on a meadowy plateau in eastern Madeira. It has long been valued as an upmarket climatic spa.

The rich merchant families of Funchal favoured the area, particularly in the 18th century, as the ideal place to build their quintas. Today, Santo da Serra is best known for the spectacular scenery of its **golf course** (►Practicalities, Sport).

What to See in Santo da Serra

Gardens close to the church in the centre of the village that originally belonged to the grounds of the Quinta do Santo da Serra have been remodelled as a public park. Today they are **popular among Madeirans and foreign visitors**. Lilies of the Nile, camellias and hydrangeas line an enchanting path through the park, which features a number of playgrounds and sports fields, as well as a small deer park. The quinta once belonged to the Blandy family: their old summer house is hidden behind hedges and tall trees.

✳
Quinta do Santo da Serra

❓ DID YOU KNOW ...?

- ... that Madeira, in Santo da Serra for example, also produces a kind of cider known as »sidra«? Well worth sampling!

▶ VISITING SANTO DA SERRA

WHERE TO EAT
► Inexpensive
A Nossa Aldeia
Sítio dos Casais Próximos
Tel. 291 552 142
Simple and hearty fare, including grilled espada

WHERE TO STAY
► Mid-range
Hotel do Santo
Sítio dos Casais Próximos

Tel. 291 550 550
Fax 291 550 559
www.enotel.com; 36 rooms
Small, pleasant hotel in the village and close to the golf course. Garden with sunbathing lawn, restaurant, bar

MARKET
Adjacent to the church, the Sunday flea market Feira da Ladra (literally: »market of the jugglers«) opens at noon.

← *They may not be particularly roomy, but the Casas de Colmo in Santana cannot be beaten for cosiness*

Miradouro dos Ingleses

✱ From the Miradouro dos Ingleses (viewpoint of the English), hewn out of the rock in the lower part of the park, it is possible to look east as far as ►Machico and the ►Ponta de São Lourenço peninsula. The miradouro earned its name by virtue of the English merchants who stationed a look-out here. When the person on watch relayed news of a trading vessel spotted on the horizon, enterprising businessmen still had enough time to hurry to Funchal in time for the docking and unloading of the ship.

✱ São Jorge

B 6

Altitude: approx. 10 – 150m/32 – 492ft   **Population:** approx. 3000

In and around São Jorge on Madeira's northern coast grow many of the osiers which are used in basketry and also play a major role in viniculture.

What to See in and Around São Jorge

Igreja de São Jorge

✱ In São Jorge stands one of the island's most remarkable churches, certainly the most beautiful of its kind on the north coast. **Dedicated to Saint George, the Baroque church** was erected on a hill to replace a 15th-century chapel that was destroyed by floods in 1660. Whilst the exterior is unostentatiously plain – a typical example of Madeiran understatement in religious architecture – the interior of the church is richly decorated with gilded woodcarvings, beautiful altarpieces and supremely artistic azulejos.

▶ VISITING SÃO JORGE

WHERE TO STAY

► **Mid-range**
Cabanas de São Jorge Village
Tel. 291 567 291, fax 291 576 032
www.cabanasvillage.com
When the tourists have departed, some 25 round bungalows provide peaceful lodgings at the viewing point.

WHERE TO EAT

► **Inexpensive**
Casa de Palha
Achada Grande (to the rear of the church)

Tel. 291 576 382
Simple snacks served in this original little eatery, a traditional wooden house

The work is arduous and anything but lucrative –
but what would the basket weavers of Camacha do without their suppliers ...

Ponta de São Jorge with its lighthouse offers fantastic views of both
the east and west coast, as it reaches far out into the ocean

Between São Jorge and Arco de São Jorge, still off the beaten track,
the Cabanas viewing point lies to the west. This is one of the most
breathtaking panoramas of the north coast. The roadhouse has an attractive terrace, whilst fruit stalls of local farms and a souvenir shop
tempt visitors to part with their cash. As almost every tourist coach
passes through here, the tranquillity of yesteryear has been sacrificed,
but São Jorge now enjoys some degree of prosperity.

✳
**Ponta de
São Jorge**

✳
**Miradouro
Cabanas**

✳ ✳ São Vicente

B 4

Altitude: approx. 15 – 350m/
49 – 1148ft

Population: approx. 6000

**São Vicente is a convenient starting point for the ascent of the Pi-
co dos Tanquinhos (1524m/5000ft) and Ruivo do Paúl (1640m/
5380ft), which provides splendid views across the mountains.**

The picturesque north coast town is located on the estuary of the Ribeira de São Vicente. A few hotels and restaurants have been built in

recent times right on the coast, but the town itself can be found a little further inland surrounded by high mountains and sheltered behind a slope – a prudent strategy to avoid the attention of pirates. In 1928, parts of São Vicente were buried by a landslide.

What to See in São Vicente

✴ **Picturesque townscape**

Altogether, São Vicente presents a harmonious appearance, not least because its inhabitants collectively took responsibility for the appearance of their houses and renovated them in the 1980s. They were rewarded with a **conservation award** and rising numbers of visitors.

✴ **Igreja de São Vicente**

The Baroque parish church, built in the 17th century, merits closer inspection. Gilded wood carvings and paintings adorn the interior, with the image of Saint Vincent adorning the ceiling. The paved square in front of the church depicts the **attributes of São Vicente**: two ravens who defended the saint's corpse and the unmanned ship from which his body was washed ashore, as legend would have it, on the south coast of Portugal.

Capela de São Roque

At the point where the Ribeira de São Vicente flows into the Atlantic, a striking rock formation reaches upwards, its summit cross visible from far out to sea. Constructed in the year 1692, the small Capela de São Roque features interesting pebble mosaics on the façade facing inland.

▶ VISITING SÃO VICENTE

WHERE TO EAT
▶ Moderate
Ferro Velho
Rua da Fonte Velha
Tel. 291 842 763
Very popular, small and cosy restaurant in the old heart of São Vicente. Good, traditional Madeiran dishes on the menu.

WHERE TO STAY
▶ Budget
Quinta Casa da Piedade
Sítio do Laranjal
Tel. 291 846 042

Fax 291 846 044; 6 rooms
Supremely attractive quinta with small, very well-tended gardens. Pleasant and friendly establishment.

Estalagem do Mar
São Vicente
Tel. 291 840 010
Fax 291 840 019, 99 rooms
Modern hotel immediately on the seafront with open air swimming pool and small indoor pool. Adjoining restaurant and a bar on the first floor which overlooks the sea.

The Grutas de São Vicente were created some 400,000 years ago as lava flows poured down from the mountains into the valley.

The caves of Sao Vicente were only opened to the public in 1996, though they were discovered much earlier. A guided tour through the imaginatively illuminated caves lasts for roughly one hour and resembles a **journey to the interior of the earth**. The caves were formed by mighty lava streams which flowed downwards from the ►Paúl da Serra region some 400,000 years ago, when Madeira's volcanoes erupted for the last time, lending the island its definitive topographical character (opening hours: 10am – 6pm daily). A new addition to the site of the caves is the **Volcanism Centre** with audio-visual presentations on the subject of volcano eruptions and the creation of an island. A garden of predominantly indigenous plants has also been created.

✷
Grutas de São Vicente

☉

Seixal

Altitude: approx. 10 – 350m/ 30 – 1148ft

Population: approx. 900

Seixal, charmingly situated on a mountainside jutting out into the ocean, is renowned for its excellent Sercial wine. Arduous labour is required to cultivate the vines here.

The land mass on which Seixal was built resembles
a paw reaching out into the ocean

Surrounded by vines Roughly halfway between ►Porto Moniz and ►São Vicente, nestling among wine terraces on the slopes of a mountain spur, lies the small settlement of Seixal. Waist-high hedges protect the tracts of land from force of the Atlantic winds.

★★ Coast road Seixal is best approached from the east, i.e. from São Vicente. This is undoubtedly the most impressive stretch of the northern coast road and **one of the most scenic routes on Madeira** altogether. The new road passes through numerous tunnels, cutting the journey time dramatically. Nevertheless, it is worth following the old coast road at least once. In some places it is reduced to a narrow, one-way thoroughfare outside the new tunnels: cut into the almost vertical cliff face, using every technical means possible and no little ingenuity, the road passes through narrow tunnels and over stone bridges, immediately above the raging surf.

★ Véu da Noiva A viewing point around 1km/half a mile east of Seixal has particularly good views of the impressive Véu da Noiva (»bridal veil«) **waterfall**, which cascades down the hillside into the ocean. Liquid refreshment can be obtained at the bar, whilst souvenirs from the shop next door.

● VISITING SEIXAL

WHERE TO STAY

▶ Budget

Brisa Mar
Sítio do Cais
Tel. 291 854 474
Fax 291 854 477; 12 rooms
Small, friendly pension, in the harbour area

WHERE TO EAT

▶ Moderate

Casa de Pasto Justiniano
Sítio Chão da Ribeira
(further inland)
Tel. 291 854 559

Espetada meat skewers served in traditional fashion: laurel twigs skewered with meat chunks are hung on a chain over the table; each guest can select his own portion. Fresh trout also on the menu

▶ Inexpensive

Brisa Mar
Sítio do Cais
Tel. 291 854 474
There is a small restaurant at the pension, a good place to sample fresh fish.

INDEX

LIST OF MAPS AND ILLUSTRATIONS

PHOTO CREDITS

PUBLISHER'S INFORMATION

Illustrations etc: 127 illustrations, 13 maps
and diagrams, one large city plan
Text: Monika I. Baumgarten, Dr. Peter H.
Baumgarten, Achim Bourmer, Heiner F.
Gstaltmayr, Dr. Eva Missler
Editing: Baedeker editorial team
(John Sykes)
Translation: Gareth Davies
Cartography: Franz Kaiser, Sindelfingen;
MAIRDUMONT/Falk Verlag, Ostfildern (city plan)
3D illustrations: jangled nerves, Stuttgart
Design: independent Medien-Design, Munich;
Kathrin Schemel

Editor-in-chief: Rainer Eisenschmid,
Baedeker Ostfildern

1st edition 2011

Based on Baedeker Allianz Reiseführer
»Madeira« 8. Auflage 2009

Copyright: Karl Baedeker Verlag, Ostfildern
Publication rights: MAIRDUMONT GmbH & Co;
Ostfildern

Printed in China

BAEDEKER GUIDE BOOKS AT A GLANCE
Guiding the World since 1827

- Andalusia
- Australia
- Austria
- Bali
- Barcelona
- Berlin
- Brazil
- Budapest
- Cape Town • Garden Route
- China
- Cologne
- Dresden
- Dubai
- Egypt
- Florence
- Florida

- France
- Gran Canaria
- Greek Islands
- Greece
- Iceland
- India
- Ireland
- Italian Lakes
- Italy
- Japan
- London
- Madeira
- Mexico
- Morocco
- Naples • Capri • Amalfi Coast
- New York

- New Zealand
- Norway
- Paris
- Portugal
- Prague
- Rome
- South Africa
- Spain
- Thailand
- Turkish Coast
- Tuscany
- Venice
- Vienna
- Vietnam

DEAR READER,

We would like to thank you for choosing this Baedeker travel guide. It will be a reliable companion on your travels and will not disappoint you.
This book describes the major sights, of course, but it also recommends hotels in the luxury and budget categories, and includes tips about where to eat or go shopping and much more, helping to make your trip an enjoyable experience. Our authors ensure the quality of this information by making regular journeys to Madeira and putting all their know-how into this book.

Nevertheless, experience shows us that it is impossible to rule out errors and changes made after the book goes to press, for which Baedeker accepts no liability. Please send us your criticisms, corrections and suggestions for improvement: we appreciate your contribution. Contact us by post or e-mail, or phone us:

▶ **Verlag Karl Baedeker GmbH**
Editorial department
Postfach 3162
73751 Ostfildern
Germany
Tel. 49-711-4502-262, fax -343
www.baedeker.com
www.baedeker.co.uk
E-Mail: baedeker@mairdumont.com